WHITEWATER RAFTING

ON

West Virginia's

New & Gauley Rivers

WHITEWATER RAFTING

ON

West Virginia's New & Gauley Rivers

COME ON IN, THE WATER'S WEIRD

JAY YOUNG

THE History PRESS

Published by The History Press
Charleston, SC 29403
www.historypress.net

First published 2011

Manufactured in the United States

ISBN 978.1.60949.246.5

Library of Congress Cataloging-in-Publication Data

Young, Jay, 1970-
Whitewater rafting on West Virginia's New & Gauley rivers : come on in, the water's weird / Jay Young.
p. cm.
Includes bibliographical references.
ISBN 978-1-60949-246-5
1. White-water canoeing--West Virginia--New River Gorge National River. 2. White-water canoeing--West Virginia--Gauley River. 3. Rafting (Sports)--West Virginia--New River Gorge National River. 4. Rafting (Sports)--West Virginia--Gauley River. 5. New River Gorge National River (W. Va.)--Guidebooks. 6. Gauley River (W. Va.)--Guidebooks. I. Title.
GV776.W42N499 2011
797.12209754--dc22
2011016279

CONTENTS

PREFACE

The problem with writing a history book is that you never know if it's complete. During the researching of *Whitewater Rafting on West Virginia's New and Gauley Rivers*, it was common to walk away from one interview with a list of multiple people with whom I should also speak. Unfortunately, there's always a clock ticking. There will always be people with whom I should have spoken but never did, and there will always be stories that should have been told but are now either lost to the past entirely or hiding just low enough under the surface as to be unnoticed.

To all those people who have all those stories, I apologize profusely! I wish I could have done better by you.

There is, however, one subject of note that I purposely left out entirely—death on the river. For months, I wavered about whether or not to put a chapter in devoted to it. And if I did, how would I approach the subject? I decided—tentatively—to go ahead and do it. I figured the best way to start was probably to pay homage to the first person who died on a commercial rafting trip, so I called Tom Dragan, who was there when it happened, and asked if he would tell me about it. Tom has been a huge help to me throughout this process as both an interview source and a gateway to other interviews.

Tom's initial answer was a flat, "No." He went on to explain a bit about why he didn't want to talk about it. In short, he felt it would be disrespectful to the person who died and to all the people who were there and live with the memory every day.

In refusing to tell me about that death, Tom helped me one more time. He convinced me once and for all that not having a chapter devoted to death on the river was a better idea. It will have to suffice to say that it happens and that the people involved carry an unimaginable burden with them for the rest of their lives. It is thankfully rare, though, and those who have seen it firsthand do an admirable job of remembering all the reasons why they love to run rivers.

ACKNOWLEDGEMENTS

I always thought that the most difficult part of winning an Oscar must be walking on stage and thanking everybody who needed thanking. I mean, my God, what happens if you walk off stage and suddenly remember you forgot to thank your mom and dad? How horrible would that be?

I'm not quite in that spot right now. For one, this isn't an Oscar; plus, I get considerably more than two minutes to remember everybody who helped me, encouraged me, reminisced about the old days with me and spent their own time researching various tidbits of history with no hope of reward. But it's a two-edged paddle. I'll feel terrible for life if I still manage to forget somebody.

If you helped me and you don't see your name here, words cannot express how profoundly sorry I am. Boy, do I ever owe you a beer.

Thank you to: Elaina Smith at New River Mountain Guides for forwarding me the timely e-mail that kicked off this whole project. Porter Jarrard, Erin Yakim, Belinda Fowler, Jamie Holt, Daniel Groves and the rest of the folks at the Vandalian Restaurant for letting me sit there and write after closing so I didn't derail my trains of thought. All my interviewees (who are listed in the bibliography) for pouring their hearts, souls and knowledge into my recorder. The National Park Service (NPS) folks at Glen Jean and Sandstone for being so excited about and behind this project. Adventures on the Gorge/Class-VI River Runners for hiring me to guide rafts and thereby setting me on this path—and for being such great interview sources. I also want to thank especially Mark Lewis from WVPRO, David Fuerst and Richard Altare of the NPS and Charlie Walbridge, all of whom helped me get a handle on the context of the whole thing early on. Thanks also to Maura Kistler, Dave Arnold, Tom Dragan, Paul Breuer and my sister, Kristan, for pre-reading this thing and offering suggestions.

Thank you tons to my loving wife, Wendy, and our dog, Louis, but not our cats. They never really supported any of this. My mother, father and sister, Dana, on the other hand, supported the heck out of it—thank you!

The psych from my editor, Joe Gartrell, at The History Press, people in the rafting industry, the National Park Service and boaters in general has been a huge source of energy for me throughout this project. Other than as mentioned in the preface, never—not once—did I bring up this book to someone or ask somebody to sit for an interview who wasn't willing to talk and who wasn't excited that somebody was going to write down the sordid tale before it's too late. I fed off that encouragement like a tree in the sunshine, and I can't thank you all enough. There are also those who helped a ton, maybe not through recorded interviews but by pointing me in the right direction and telling me, sometimes emphatically, what they felt this book needed to include. Thank you also to Jaime Muehl at The History Press, who had the misfortune of copyediting my hackery. That sentence this good is is because Jaime. Heh.

Lastly, my time on the water and the friends with whom I've spent it have enriched my life immeasurably. Hopefully, with this book I can begin to repay some of that.

Prologue

SWEET'S FALLS, PART I

"Sometimes you get to see a show. Other times, you *are* the show."

A grizzled veteran raft guide told me that once, as I sat dejectedly in Chetty's Pub at Class-VI River Runners watching the video of the day's raft trip on the New River.

In the video, I—a first-year guide as wet behind the ears as a baby fish—am falling out of my own raft, abandoning, as it were, my paying guests and leaving them to the mercy of the raging water. But hey, at least they're still in the boat. On the Jumbotron, I flip backward over the side of the raft, and my feet point to the sky as if to say, "Hi clouds!" In an instant, I disappear into the murky depths, doomed to spend the next few seconds wearing a dunce cap in Davey Jones's locker. The video boater who shot the stunning footage was kind enough to reverse its direction, so onscreen I pop out of the water and back into my seat, only to relive it again and again.

Everybody in the bar—and it was mercilessly crowded—roared with laughter. As is the tradition, I swam, so I bought a round of beer for all the other guides on the trip. It was while hoisting one of those in toast that my venerable friend uttered his words of wisdom.

Oddly enough, I found it reassuring. It means, essentially, that anything can happen to any boat in any rapid on any river. Every whitewater boater, no matter how experienced, is at constant risk of becoming the show.

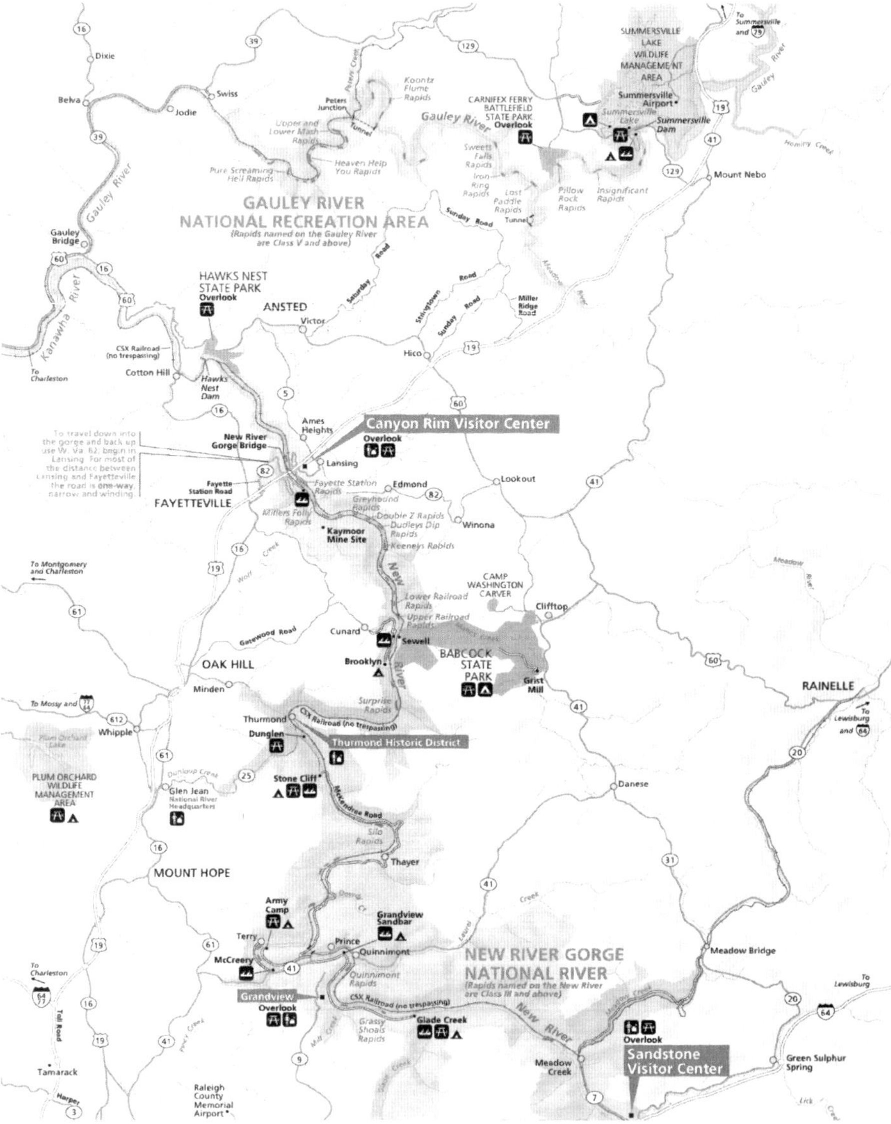

Map of the New and Gauley Rivers region. *National Park Service Collection.*

Months later, my friend's counsel replayed itself in my mind as I perched safely on Video Rock on the left bank of the Gauley River at a Class-V rapid called Sweet's Falls. Sweet's is a fourteen-foot-tall, forty-foot-long slide. The normal raft line down the falls is actually pretty easy to run, but the water drops so steeply that it's difficult to judge where you are until it's almost too late. If a boat misses to the right, it slides into the Energizer Hole—a roiling, recirculating, aerated pile of whitewater. Miss it to the left and the boat will slam into Dildo Rock, so called because when a boat hits it, that boat is, well, let's just say it's in trouble.

I had just run Sweet's Falls myself, but in a private boat—not guiding. Thankfully, I was not the show. Giddily, mischievously and perhaps a bit guiltily, however, I hoped to see one.

I was not alone. Around me, above me on the rocks and across the river there were hundreds of other onlookers. They were hikers, raft guides, other private boaters, raft guests who were thrilled to have survived thus far and, like vultures, video boaters. We didn't want anybody to get hurt. That would be horrible. But it would be a lie to say that the vast majority of us didn't want one thing: carnage. Mayhem on the water sells videos, and most video boaters work at least partially on commission, so they especially longed for a good show. Thankfully, there is no shortage of carnage at Sweet's. Google it if you don't believe me. It's all there.

From my comfy seat, I watched a flotilla of boats approach.

The first few made it through the falls cleanly, but one of them, a sixteen-foot raft, wasn't so lucky. Slamming into the unstable water at the bottom of the drop, three of the nine people fell right out.

The slide was past, but the fun was just beginning. In the wide swath of current immediately below the falls, there's a rock called Postage Due, so named for a raft's tendency to get stamped and stuck on it if it hits broadside. The cleanest line is to the right of Postage Due, but deprived of almost half her boat's power and distracted as she attempted to pull her guests back into the boat, the guide seemed oblivious that she, her boat and her guests were all headed left into a tight channel with a ninety-degree turn called the Box Canyon. A sixteen-footer can make it through the Box if it manages to squirt to the right of a boulder in the center called Pyramid Rock. The move there, however, is technical. It takes a very well-timed paddle stroke from the guide, who just then wasn't paying attention. She missed it. From there, it's a fairly safe bet that a boat will get stuck in an eddy from which it's quite difficult to escape. In a fleeting moment, the guide and her boat were there.

Sweet's Falls, Gauley River—too far left. *Whitewater Photography.*

By that time, there were more paddles under and around the boat than in it. She tried in vain to push the boat out, but it was a lost cause. The cameras were rolling. The video boaters smelled cash.

Upstream, a boat hit Dildo Rock head on. The raft folded in on itself like a giant rubber taco shell, and people exploded from it in all directions, like sparks from a skyrocket. Nine people, all of them in the water, drifted left toward the Box Canyon and our first boat, which was still stuck there.

It wasn't the worst-case scenario, but hey, the moment wasn't over. Several swimmers drifted under the raft, which is about eightish on a one-to-ten scale of bad. There is no air under the raft. Up until then, it was all just good clean fun.

Video boaters frantically screamed instructions to the stuck guide. "Get them! Get them in the boat!" She reacted quickly, and soon everybody was safe. Some swimmers made it into the boat, while others were flushed under it and through a body-width slot in the rocks called the Poop Shoot.

The crowd roared like Romans in the Coliseum.

Rafting on the New and Gauley Rivers in south central West Virginia sure didn't begin that way. In the earliest days of rafting in the region, a boater could get downright lonely out there. And as one might expect, the journey from those days to now is an odd one, as turbulent and thrilling as any raft ride.

So how exactly did we get from there to here? I blame George Washington.

Ere There Was Rubber

On the morning of November 29, 1812, U.S. Supreme Court chief justice John Marshall climbed into his boat, a sixty-foot bateaux, and shivered against the chill. Long, lanky and clad in a mix of skins and wool, his belly still full from breakfast, Marshall peered ahead past the islands, among which the team had camped, and into the New River Gorge in what is now southern West Virginia.

Almost three months earlier, Marshall had begun his expedition with high hopes of finding a navigable waterway between Virginia and the Ohio Territory. The roots of the expedition can be traced to George Washington himself, who viewed the Ohio River Valley as only tenuously, if at all, tied to the fortunes of the United States. To remedy the situation, Washington urged strong economic ties to Ohio.

Such ties would require a commerce route, and Washington had two in mind: the Potomac and James Rivers. Waterways were king for moving goods because they often required little improvement, and boats were, relatively speaking, high tech compared to available forms of overland travel. A boat could move bigger loads more quickly. In 1785, again at Washington's urging, the young nation spawned two companies to explore such possibilities: the Potomac Company and the James River Company.

Marshall served in the Continental army under Washington and was also his trusted friend and advisor, so it is unremarkable that he shared the president's vision.

Of course, this doesn't quite fully explain why the chief justice of the U.S. Supreme Court decided to lead a dangerous expedition down what is today still considered a challenging run, especially against the backdrop of the War of 1812, which Congress declared only three months prior to the voyage's start. It may, however, be helpful to consider what is conspicuously missing from Marshall's River Commission Report—namely, that very same war. Its absence is especially odd, considering the obvious military advantages such an artery would yield. Perhaps, rather than embarking on his journey *because* of the war, he went in spite of it.

After all, Marshall was so personally invested in the endeavor that it's likely that even the war couldn't hold him back. Not only had he been behind Washington's vision from the get go, but he was also a major stockholder of both the Potomac and James River Companies. So, when Virginia's General Assembly chose commissioners to survey the headwaters of the James, Greenbrier and New Rivers, it's probable that Marshall, even at fifty-seven years of age, leapt at the opportunity to exert his political clout for an appointment.

As he sat and waited for his first glimpse of the mighty New River, Marshall may have reflected on his journey up until then. The expedition began on the first of September in Lynchburg, Virginia. The team made its way up the James and then the Jackson River to the mouth of Dunlop's Creek at what is now Covington, Virginia, surveying all the way. At the mouth of Dunlop's Creek, the expedition loaded its boat and supplies onto wagons and pulled them over the Allegheny Mountains to the mouth of Howard's Creek on the Greenbrier River, where even now there is a bateaux landing.

A loaded bateaux drafted only up to eighteen inches of water, but even so, the expedition had trouble in the shallow waters of the Greenbrier. In his River Commission Report, Marshall laments the water level:

> *The season had been remarkably dry, and the water was declared by the inhabitants to be as low as at any period within their recollection…The labour of removing stones, and of dragging the boat over those which could not be removed without implements provided for the purpose, was so great that your Commissioners at one time were enabled to advance*

> *only three miles in two days, even with the assistance of a horse and of many additional laborers.*

Almost at once, it was obvious to Marshall that he and his team would not experience similar problems on the upcoming leg of their journey. When he saw the much higher water of the New River, Marshall may have even wondered if the bateau was up to the task. It would have been a smart thing to ponder. Bateaux had plied the waters of the New River upstream of the Greenbrier confluence before, but never had such a boat even attempted to run the Lower New River Gorge, which is still considered a challenging run by today's standards.

Other than that both are boats, a bateau is nothing like a modern raft. Made of wood planks with cotton stuffed in the cracks, bateaux leaked like sieves and required constant bailing. In the neighborhood of sixty feet long, seven to eight feet wide and pointed at both bow and stern, bateaux are poled in shallow water and swept and steered with a broad rudder in deep water. Narrow walkways along each gunwale accommodated a bateau's two polemen. Standing on the walkway near the boat's bow, a poleman would plant his pole among the rocks at the bottom of the river and then walk sternward with the pole braced on a rawhide chest harness. A captain stood constant watch near the bow to

National Park Service Collection.

guide the sweeper with hand signals. Some bateaux also had a smaller sweep near the bow, so the captain could affect a quick turn if necessary.

Bateaux were typically captained and crewed by slaves. More than one amateur historian theorizes that this may be due to the extreme danger of poling and sweeping such a behemoth, loaded with a few tons of tobacco and maybe a cow or two, through whitewater.

As any modern boatman or boatwoman on the New River can attest, the river's surface in a rapid has a topography to it that virtually never allows a straight line sixty feet long. The water slips over rocks and around bends, creating waves and troughs, pillows and hydraulics. Therein lies the genius of a boat that was otherwise utterly unsuited to the Lower New River Gorge—it flexes to absorb some of the roiling geometry of the river.

Still, a bateau in the Lower Gorge is virtually a recipe for disaster. Bateaumen needed a level of skill that probably hasn't been seen on the New River since. Raft guides may disagree, but the difference between paddling an inflated rubber tube and a sixty-foot collection of planks cannot be slight.

Nevertheless, it's obvious from Marshall and company's River Commission Report that the water level in the New River ended up being mostly to their liking, especially when compared to the Greenbrier.

Eventually, Marshall made it to Kanawha (ken-AW) Falls, where he and his party left their boat and traveled home.

Marshall's expedition was the first in recorded history to successfully navigate the entire New River Gorge by boat. Travel on the New River, however, dates farther back than Europeans in America, when native tribes plied its waters above and below the gorge. It may be that Native Americans did run the Lower Gorge, but there is understandably no recorded evidence to support this. And indeed, some Native Americans called the New River *Mondongachate* (mon-DON-ga-cha-TEH), which, loosely translated, means "River of Death."

Throughout most of the 1800s, bateaux plied the New River above and below the Lower Gorge, and a few times, a daring expedition would make its way into the canyon. In each instance, such expeditions undertook survey operations. But gradually, the objects of such surveys turned from canals and waterway travel to a railroad. During those years, nothing was organized to improve the New River.

Then war again came to the New River Valley. At the start of the Civil War, Confederate troops moved into the area, and development of the New River as a military supply line became a priority. Confederate major Thomas L. Brown led the effort to improve the river, but it's not clear that his efforts ever reached the Lower Gorge. By the time the war was over, many of the improvements the Confederacy was able to complete had been washed away.

Halfhearted and ill-fated attempts to improve the New River, including for steamboat travel, continued for some time, but none amounted to anything other than upgrades that were relatively small scale when compared to Washington and Marshall's grand vision, and none was in the formidable Lower Gorge.

After the war, work resumed on the railroad. Money, however, was in short supply, and the Chesapeake & Ohio (C&O) Railway asked C.P. Huntington, who had just completed the first transcontinental railway, the Central Pacific, to finance the project. Before agreeing to do so, Huntington wanted to see the route for himself, so in 1869, he set off to do just that. From Hinton to Hawk's Nest, his voyage was entirely by bateau.

William and Joe Hinton and a third man named Parker Adkins hired themselves out to guide the boat. The trip was successful, and Huntington must have been sufficiently impressed. Shortly after, surveyors arrived to thoroughly map out the line, and work on the C&O Railway began in earnest.

For a while, railroad builders employed bateaux to assist, but the practice was abandoned quickly. It was simply too dangerous in the Lower Gorge. "Since the building of the railroad was begun," wrote Charles Nordhoff in 1871, "several men have been drowned in the river; and lately all the boats on the lower part have been destroyed by the contractors who at first used them, because they found their use too dangerous to life."

Shortly after the railroad was complete, in his *Scribner's Monthly* article "New Ways in the Old Dominion" (1873), Jed Hotchkiss further described the strange relationship between railroad and bateaux. "Two years ago it was impossible to even ride through the long cañon on horseback," he wrote. "And the only way in which it could be seen was by means of the long, narrow, arrowy batteaux, and their skillful masters even at times hesitated to shoot the more impetuous rapids. [For the surveyors] hanging from cliffs eighty or a hundred feet above the water, batteaux [*sic*] were in most cases useless."

"When the contractors went to work," Hotchkiss continued,

> *they, of course, needing larger quantities of supplies, employed the river boats to bring them; but even they had to transport everything from a few landings, on horse's backs; they brought boats, and used them until several men were drowned; and so treacherous is the river that it was presently found necessary to absolutely forbid the men to bathe in it.*

There is little, if any, evidence to suggest that anybody ran the Lower Gorge at all immediately after the C&O was complete. Why on earth would they risk life, limb and cargo to move a ton of tobacco in those treacherous waters when they could more easily drop twenty times that into a railroad car?

It is possible, but exceptionally unlikely given the deaths on the river during railroad construction, that whitewater tourism actually has its roots in that time. One passage in particular in Hotchkiss's article may support this. If not, it certainly is startling in its accuracy:

> *The adventurous and enterprising tourist, if hereafter there shall remain such a being, may make the tour of the New River cañon; as voyages by canoe are just now fashionable, we do not doubt that some romantic voyagers will make this attempt. They are hereby warned that it is an exciting and in some parts even perilous passage, through a long succession of rapids, for which even the passenger needs good nerves.*

Of course, modern raft runs would be vastly different from an early bateau survey expedition in more ways than just the boat. In fact, those expeditions, which typically followed the river past its confluence with the Gauley, were the only since—and possibly forever more—to run every rapid in the Lower Gorge.

A typical Lower New River run today ends at Fayette Station or continues another mile-plus to Teay's Landing. Boaters thereby take out before having to stroke through the oceanic expanse of Hawk's Nest Lake. That reservoir formed behind the Hawk's Nest

Dam, which workers completed for hydroelectric power in the 1930s. Along with the dam, Union Carbide bore a tunnel through Gauley Mountain to divert the New River through the plant to a point three miles downstream.

That tunnel is synonymous with the worst industrial disaster in American history. Though Union Carbide eventually admitted to 109 worker deaths from inhaling silicon dust, a congressional hearing determined that the number killed was actually 476. Even that, however, is almost definitely an understatement. Many of the nearly 3,000 workers traveled to West Virginia for the job and then left upon falling sick, so it's impossible to determine exactly how many died. Some estimates are closer to one-third of all workers.

The much lesser issue of Hawk's Nest Dam—the one that concerns modern boaters—is twofold.

First, the diverted water left behind a drained section of riverbed forever to be known as the Dries. Hawk's Nest Dam occasionally releases water into the Dries, but only when the volume becomes high enough that the tunnel can't keep up with it. When that happens, boaters flock to the Dries. But at all other times, it's quite…dry.

The second minor tragedy is that the reservoir behind the dam quickly flooded over every rapid in that section of river, never to be seen or run again. No descriptions of those rapids exist, so it's impossible to know what's there. But considering the quality of whitewater above and below Hawk's Nest Lake and Dam, it's easy to imagine a magnificent section of challenging water, much like the rest of the Lower Gorge.

Evidence to the contrary is in short supply, and many historians consider the last complete bateaux run through the Lower New River Gorge to be C.P. Huntington's railroad survey in 1869. If that's true, then apparently it was eighty-eight years before anybody ran it again.

Bob "Dog" Underwood worked for Wildwater Unlimited Expeditions and was one of the first professional raft guides to ply the Lower New River. He grew up at the top of the Lower Gorge in a town called Thurmond, and he remembers attempts on the Lower Gorge being few and far between. "Occasionally, growing up I would see a canoe or two go by, maybe an old army raft," he recounted. "But it was maybe once in two, three years, something like that. I had seen some of them go and never saw them again, and I had seen some of them walk out again without their equipment."

Underwood, a lifelong West Virginian, had himself made a few tentative, ill-fated forays downstream. He was ten years old in 1953 when he and some friends made their first attempt at the Lower Gorge on a homemade raft, a basic wooden rectangle about ten feet long and two feet wide. "We'd get old boards from some of the old buildings and build a little raft or boat, and run it as far as we could," said Underwood. "Usually it was low water, so we didn't run any big stuff. We'd run far enough to be interesting, and then we'd let the boats go and walk back."

"We would carry inner tubes with us," he continued. "That was our life jacket. If something happened, we'd hang on to the inner tube, let the boat go and swim to shore."

In 1957, John Berry and Bob Harrigan were at the cutting edge of American paddling. The two men initiated decked boating in America when they stretched a tarp over the gunwales of an open canoe, and they even designed an early C2 (a kayak-like, two-person canoe). Many boaters credit Berry with the first ever Eskimo roll of a C2's smaller cousin, a C1.

Together, Barry and Harrigan pioneered run after run on mid-Atlantic rivers, including sections of the Youghiogheny River in Pennsylvania and the Cheat River in West Virginia. True to form, they also teamed up Labor Day Weekend in 1957 to run the New River from Thurmond to Fayette Station. Not much is known about the water level that day, but it's difficult for a modern raft guide to imagine the run being too gnarly at that time of year.

Twenty miles up the road, another river coursed along a tight gorge. Of smaller volume, but steeper descent in a tighter channel, the Gauley patiently awaited its own first descent.

Though West Virginia is known mainly for its vast coal resources, if you look far enough back in its history, say to the late 1700s and early 1800s, you'll also find a thriving salt industry. Such an industry created a demand for other natural resources, most notably—insofar as Gauley River boaters are concerned—wood. The coal boom of the late 1800s and early 1900s powered the Industrial Revolution, but it also upped the demand for wood to a frenzied level. The coal industry needed homes, churches, barns and company buildings by the thousands, and the Gauley River had wood aplenty to supply them.

Soon, a bona fide wood rush of the Gauley and Meadow Rivers was on. The year 1883 saw the first big log drive on the Gauley River, and by 1885, the timber industry was in full swing. As loggers hewed their way up the Gauley from its confluence with the New River, a typical log's watery journey grew longer and longer. The Gauley, however, would not cooperate easily. Downstream of what modern boaters consider to be "the Gauley," the federal government sponsored the digging of a one-hundred-foot-wide channel through which to float logs, but timber companies still needed more. At some point in the 1880s, timber companies began to dynamite sluices where large ledges wouldn't permit logs to pass. Lost Paddle, Iron Ring and Sweet's Falls are just three of the rapids that exist as they are today, not due to nature's entropic march, but because men packed them full of dynamite and blew them to bits.

Like the rapids buried forever under the surface of Hawk's Nest Lake on the New River, we'll never know what the dynamited ledges of the Gauley River looked like or whether whitewater rafting as an industry would have been viable on them.

Some may say that rafts would have been impractical on a ledge-filled river with the volume and gradient of the Gauley, especially in the case of Lost Paddle, but the point is academic. Ledges were sliced into sluices, and eventually the rafts came.

Interlude

BROKEN ROSE

The bateau *Rose of Nelson* was in trouble. Broached as it was against the rocks in the middle of a Class-IV rapid called Dudley's Dip in the Lower Gorge of the New River, it took on water about as quickly as one might expect of a forty-three-and-a-half-foot-long wooden bucket.

Its crew tried valiantly to bail it. They heaved water from the *Rose*'s hull into the river like a bucket brigade dowsing a fire, but to no avail. Within moments, the bateau tipped upstream and exposed its innards to the rushing torrent. Pinned and swamped, it flexed around the rocks. It held for a brief second, which to its crew must have seemed like an hour, and then finally fell apart, sending splintered wood and the crew into the drink.

The year was 2004.

In 2003, to celebrate the twenty-fifth anniversary of the New River Gorge National River, the Park Service organized a reenactment of C.P. Huntington's 1869 voyage.

At the time of the reenactment, however, the New River ran at flood levels. The water gauge at Fayette Station read twenty feet. Contrary to popular belief, neither the NPS nor the industry as a whole dictates a "cutoff" level past which no commercial rafting will occur, but a relatively low twelve feet, which is itself a huge volume of water, is the unofficial guideline. Before it even reached the Lower Gorge, the *Rose of Nelson* braved standing waves up to seven feet tall with little to protect it but a six-inch bulkhead its builders installed to help it shed water.

Against waves that large, though, the bulkheads did little, and the boat swamped regularly.

Every night and often throughout each day, the *Rose* eddied out for repairs. Its crew pounded cotton into the spaces between planks in a futile effort to keep the river out of the boat. When camping at night, they purposely swamped the bateau to keep its boards swollen and tight.

But as it approached the town of Thurmond, everybody aboard the *Rose* had the same thought: "There's no way we'll make it through the Lower Gorge." Prudence won the day, and instead of trying, the team removed the *Rose* from the water and dried it out for a rain date with the New River.

That day finally arrived a year later, when the *Rose* again put in at Thurmond and headed into the gorge. The first half of the journey from Thurmond to Fayette Station is relatively calm. There is only one significant rapid, a Class III called Surprise, and the *Rose of Nelson* made it through easily to the delight of everybody aboard.

The *Rose of Nelson* hits the hole in Surprise rapid on the Lower New River during a 2004 NPS bateau reenactment. Captain Mike Neal of the Virginia Canal Society works the stern sweep, while Dewey Wood, who died tragically in a 2007 shooting, mans the bow. *National Park Service Collection.*

Though they had to stop often to effect repairs, the crew of the *Rose* watched rapid after rapid disappear around the bends behind them. One of those is a rapid called Lower Keeney. Together with Upper and Middle Keeney Rapids, Lower Keeney forms one of two Class-V drops, but only at higher water levels when they blend into one long flume. That day, the New River flowed low enough to give it a go.

Deftly, the crew maneuvered the *Rose of Nelson* to river left (the left side of the river as a boater faces downstream) in the calm pool above Lower Keeney. Once lined up for the rapid, they paused to let the river push them where they needed to be. They hovered over the entrance to the drop and took in the roiling path stretched out below. Both banks were lined with spectators cheering them on.

The *Rose* dove into the first waves, and the bateau flexed and bent to absorb the rise and fall of the river. In a moment that passed all too quickly, it was through. The crowd erupted in cheers.

Next up, the crew knew, would be Dudley's Dip, a rocky dogleg left. Dudley's is a wide-open green highway at some water levels but would be

Cliff Bobinski of the NPS deals with the aftermath of the 2004 bateau reenactment. *National Park Service Collection.*

steeper and more difficult that day, so the crew eddied out once again for repairs. They spent hours plugging leaks, sometimes with people in the water with masks and snorkels trying to locate the many tiny gaps that had developed throughout the day.

Finally, with the boat as plugged as it could be, they pushed off and headed downstream.

Cliff Bobinski, a ranger working out of the Glen Jean Park Headquarters, rowed up alongside the bateau, running safety for the crew in case the worst happened. Bobinski recommended a clean line to them. "Enter right of center," he advised. "And then turn back left with the current to split the difference between two rocks." He watched in horror, however, as the boat floated exactly the opposite way, entering too far left. Instead of turning left with the current, the panicked crew forced the bateau right—broadside to the current—which swept it against the rocks.

The event marked the sudden end of the reenactment, which was itself historic. Bobinski spent the rest of the afternoon and much of the next day picking up pieces of the *Rose of Nelson*.

THE RODMAN EXPEDITION

Perhaps fittingly for the most challenging big-water river in its region, the Gauley did not give up its first descent easily. It fought kicking and screaming by nature of its difficulty and its obscurity relative to the New River.

Tucked away in a winding, inaccessible gorge, the Gauley flowed unknown to all but local non-boaters and fishermen until well into the 1950s, when Ray Moore of Alexandria, Virginia, found it. In 1959, he invited a few friends from the Washington, D.C. area, plus two from Pittsburgh, to attempt a run.

One of those Pittsburgh paddlers was Sayre Rodman. Rodman and his wife, Jean, were accomplished rafters and apprentices to Moore. "He taught Jean and me what he knew about rafts, short-fused dynamite sticks, and other subjects where one should pay close attention," Rodman wrote in the April 1987 edition of the *Highlands Voice*, a newsletter that the West Virginia Highlands Conservancy publishes monthly. (I actually stumbled across a reprinting of that article by Dave Elkinton, also in the *Highlands Voice*, this time in December 2006.)

The rafts Moore taught the Rodmans about were odd boats, indeed. There were few, if any, companies making rafts specifically for whitewater at the time, so they cut their teeth in jury-rigged army Air Corps surplus boats. The boats were twelve feet long, six feet wide and designed to be paddled by six people. The Rodmans glued flexible oarlocks midway

Doug Proctor inflates Jean Rodman's Gauley raft, *Hard Hoe. J. Young.*

along the outer tubes and adopted a western style of rowing. As with most things jiggered, the boats needed repairs often. The Rodmans reportedly went through more than their share of glue and duct tape. Without a rigid rowing frame attached to their boats, they soon added their own techniques to their repertoires, bouncing off rocks to change direction and even tipping boats onto their sides to slip through some of the narrower channels.

The Rodmans rowed their boats into more history than just the Gauley River, by the way. Boaters also credit them with first descents on the Youghiogheny and early descents on the Cheat River.

The group put in at Route 39, east of Summersville, and encountered its first serious whitewater at the old Route 19 crossing, which is now submerged permanently under the waters of Summersville Lake. "The river was sort of high; out of its banks," said Rodman. "We soon were in the woods, lining around rapids, laboriously roping from tree to tree in water over our heads. The owner of a house along the river took pity on the sodden group, and sheltered us for the night. He talked bitterly about the proposed dam, which would one day drown all his land."

"We made a few more miles the next day, but it wasn't much fun," Rodman continued. "One shaken man said that his big raft did an ender cleanly over his head. Fortunately, Ray's guys were good at re-entering their rafts via the bailing-bucket roper. Totally exhausted, we camped just above the dam site." Except for Ray—and he only halfheartedly—the group was ready to call it a weekend. The going was simply too rough, and the next day, Rodman bushwhacked, hitchhiked and finally returned with their car from the proposed takeout point. "I'd already learned that, on Ray's exploratory runs, you bring topo maps and pack frames. With enough psychological drive, you can hump out two deflated rafts per trip. Ah, youth. Gauley: 1, boaters: 0."

Rodman thought of the magnificent Gauley River often over the next two years. Then, one dreary day in May 1961, he and Jean, plus Ralph

Someplace high upstream from the current Summersville Dam site, the crew from Pittsburgh prepares to put in on the first descent of the Gauley River. *Sayre Rodman.*

and Kay Krichbaum and Ken Hawker, returned to try again. Simply getting to the river proved to be no mean feat. "We had shuttled a car down near Swiss somewhere," said Jean. "Ralph and his wife, Kay, had forgotten their PFDs and had to find a store that sold the old horse-collar orange life jackets. There were no interstates or three-lane roads in those days, so it all took a lot of time."

The group sat out a brief snowstorm under the Route 19 bridge and then set out in water Rodman estimated to be in the neighborhood of fifteen hundred cubic feet per second, or cfs. Rodman described that momentous day in nearly giddy terms. The group, he wrote, "ran superb water the rest of the day, and camped precisely under the present dam. Not many people have run that part. Take the best of the rapids on the Cheat run below Albright; add many more; pack them into shorter distance. A few gentlemen's Class V's, nothing really hairy. I remember it as much better than the part below Sweet's Falls. We enjoyed it, immensely."

The next day dawned sunny, and "the run to the Meadow River was just fun. We'd earlier scouted a big one below Carnifex Ferry, big waves

On the first descent of the Gauley River, 1961, Sayre Rodman lines up for an unnamed rapid that is currently submerged under Summersville Lake. *Ralph Krichbaum.*

Sayre Rodman hits the meat of an unnamed rapid currently submerged under Summersville Lake. *Ralph Krichbaum.*

but no problem. Below the Meadow, we quickly saw things were getting more interesting. The first serious rapids ate one of my oars."

In his *Highland Voice* article, Rodman described what happened to Kay Krichbaum at a rapid now known as Iron Ring. Of course, modern Gauley boaters probably aren't too surprised to read that it was the hairiest moment of the trip. Though most people don't find the standard line through Iron Ring to be especially difficult, many feel the consequences for blowing it are some of the most severe on the river. A lot of water flows into a cave formed by a large, overhanging slab of rock on the right bank, and it doesn't take a genius to understand that that's a bad, bad place to go.

"Kay's boat stalled upstream," Rodman wrote,

> *and vanished, like a fly taken by a trout, in mid-river. A remarkable lady, she dove, making the snap decision that going thru a hole ahead of a big raft is better than the alternative. We, including her husband, watched the downstream* [sic], *as did her 6 by 12 foot raft with oars still intact in the oarlocks. Twice she had come up in the dark, and grabbed a*

Ken Hawker all turned around at Iron Ring rapid. Moments later, the same squirrelly water that spun Hawker would pull Kay Krichbaum under and into the cave on river right. *Sayre Rodman.*

> *breath. Behind the long slab leaning on the bank, river right, flows a lot of water. In hindsight we might have read the surface currents better.*

Kay eventually floated out from the cave, but shaken by the events at Iron Ring, the group decided to walk past what is now called Sweet's Falls.

They camped on a sandbar downstream, and Rodman wrote:

> *The last day was brilliant and clear, and the purple rhododendron was in bloom along the canyon walls. For a while, we had good fast water to enjoy, with nothing to worry Kay, who felt a tad cautious now. When we hit the quieter water above Swiss, we knew we'd had three memorable days.*
>
> *Jean and I have had worthwhile outings in nice places. Consider first seeing the tip of Mount Everest by moonlight on New Year's Eve from Tyangboche Monastery. The first Gauley run was about that good.*

WILDWATER UNLIMITED

In 1995, at the peak of West Virginia's commercial whitewater activity, 225,000 raft customers whooped and hollered down the New and Gauley Rivers with steely-eyed raft guides behind them pushing rubber. There were days that year when a person could almost cross the river walking on rafts and never get wet. It was hard to believe that at the start of 1968, the number was closer to zero.

We can trace the roots of whitewater rafting in America to the 1800s, when the first rubber boats hit the water. While the earliest known commercial whitewater trips occurred in the latter part of the century, John D. Rockefeller Jr. created the first real river outfitter in 1956 on the Snake River under the shadow of the Grand Tetons. The public met his Grand Teton Lodge Company with a resounding yawn, but within a handful of years, they warmed to the idea. Following the lead of Rockefeller Jr., commercial river runners sprang up all over the western half of the United States. The East was soon to follow as outfitters appeared along the banks of a handful of rivers, including the Youghiogheny in Pennsylvania.

It is there where the story of commercial rafting in West Virginia really takes off. In November 1968, an unassuming but ambitious young couple moved from the Youghiogheny to the New River Gorge. Jon Dragan and Melanie Campbell would go on to birth an industry.

In one of his summers away from college, Jon worked for the Red Cross in Pennsylvania, teaching canoeing in its whitewater safety

Jon Dragan sets shuttle for a run on the Youghiogheny River in Pennsylvania. *Butch Christian Collection.*

program. "That was where he really decided that he wanted to spend most of his life around water," said Tom "Slick" Dragan, Jon's younger brother by six years. "We were very fortunate, in that our parents traveled. They took us different places. We were just into canoeing and swimming, hiking and all that other stuff, and it was the natural progression over to whitewater rafting. There was no lightning bolt. It was a very slow progression over time." Eventually, Jon found his way to Wilderness Voyagers, an outfitter on the Youghiogheny River, where he worked as a guide and helped the owners, Lance and Lee Martin, run their business.

Lee Martin was also a Girl Scout canoe instructor. She had taught Melanie to paddle and invited her to join the organization, where she met Jon. "He was my knight in shining armor," said Melanie. The two worked together often and grew fond of each other quickly.

An athletic, sandy-haired young man with an iron will, Jon soon became restless working for the Martins. He wanted to start his own company. It was the popular wisdom, however, that the "Yough" was full. "People didn't feel that there was enough there for another family to be included in it," said Melanie. In addition, though Jon and Lance worked together well enough, they were sometimes at odds.

Melanie Dragan, wife of the late Jon Dragan and mayor of Thurmond (population six), at her home next to the river that drew her and Jon to a depressed little corner of West Virginia to birth an industry. *J. Young.*

"The way I knew Lance," said Tom, "he was laid back." Both men were heavily into the outdoors, adventuring and having fun, but

> *Jon was aggressive. And I don't mean that in a negative way. It's just that when he saw something, he went after it. He did it as well as it could be done, and he did it because he made up his mind to do it. It's as simple as that. They were two different people without a doubt.*
>
> *That's probably one of the reasons he ended up coming down South. I don't think they would have ever worked well together long term. Short term, they both liked the river. Both were into good times. But as far as their business plans went—much different.*

In 1967, Jon asked Melanie if she wanted to have a look at a river in West Virginia. Jon remembered running one a couple years earlier with John Sweet and a group of old C1-ers. "The Olympians," Melanie called them. The group may have included John Berry and Bob Harrigan. "I said, sure, why not? What have we got to lose?"

The pair set out for the New River in southern West Virginia, but Jon wasn't exactly certain where to put in or, for that matter, where the river was on a map. They drove into Fayette County on State Route 19 and finally entered the New River Gorge near the town of Prince. Jon pulled out his map, but the two still didn't get their bearings until they spied a sign that said, "Thurmond 16 miles." Still not entirely certain of whether or not they were even close to an appropriate put-in, but enjoying the adventure nonetheless, Jon and Melanie bumped their way down a dirt road in his pickup truck through the town of Thayer.

"On the other side of Thayer," said Melanie, "we met a man named Shorty. He was a little guy. He lived in Thayer, and he was making his way to Mr. Pugh's Grocery Store, which was in the Dunglen building," on the other side of the river from Thurmond. From his grocery alongside

Jon Dragan on the New River, 1969. *Dragan Collection.*

the New River, Mr. Pugh sold basic food and fishing supplies and had a number of small shacks, which he rented to anglers.

Jon and Melanie realized that the town was about midway along the river. "Jon went in and talked to Mr. Pugh and came back out and said, 'Hey, he'll rent us one of these little fishing shacks for five dollars a month.' I said, 'Take it!' and we paid for a year's worth."

The next summer, Jon brought Tom, who was fresh out of high school, down for a look and "just to run the river and have fun," he said.

"I think in the back of Jon's mind, he had every intention of coming down here and doing something," said Tom. "He was looking for someplace to go, where he could do a whitewater raft trip." However, "I don't *know* that. This is all hindsight, because we never talked about it in our family. We just did things."

"I really thought the Upper New was boring and almost didn't come back," Tom continued. Then, they ran the Lower New. "I said, okay, this is good."

Jon was hooked on the water in the New River and the wild area through which it flowed. He was also entirely smitten with the area's unique coal history. The very next winter, Jon and Melanie came back for good and incorporated Wildwater Expeditions Unlimited before the New Year.

Wildwater bought two rafts, which were manufactured in West Virginia by a company called Rubber Fabricators. "There was no special design," said Tom. "There were two Green River boats. We called them *One Paw* and *Two Paw*, because we took them up to my dad's shop to paint them, and Jon had a St. Bernard. He stepped in a paint can, and put his paw down on the boat. Jon's boat was *One Paw*, my boat was *Two Paw* and that was it."

In their first season of operation, many of their customers were friends and relatives. It was also easier to get customers from the Pittsburgh area because, one, Jon and Melanie knew people there and two, Pittsburgh people knew about the Youghiogheny River. Many had paddled with Wilderness Voyagers and were looking for something bigger and better.

"But the numbers weren't there," explained Tom. "A trip with ten people…there were four of us as guides—Jon, myself, Chris [Jon and Tom's younger brother], Mel and friends; Mel's brother and sister. We probably had more guides than we did customers."

Wildwater Expeditions Unlimited guides prepare near the foot of the Summersville Dam for a Gauley trip, circa 1971. *Dragan Collection.*

"We weren't in it to make money." continued Tom. "We weren't in it to *lose* money, but it was more of a summer thing to do. You cut grass and run raft trips. You put a couple bucks in your pocket. We were also working for my dad during the school year. He had a construction company, so we were making money there. It was *never* about the money."

Jon soon made friends in the West Virginia Department of Tourism, however, and managed to tag along with members of that office to several tourism expos. Jon and Melanie would pay their own way on the trips but could hand out Wildwater brochures, which at the time were simple mimeographed sheets. "We had nothing fancy," said Melanie. "In 1970, my mom was the director of the Pittsburgh vocational schools, so they printed our first color brochure. It was something for the kids to experience." Melanie also found work as a teacher north of Pittsburgh, and between that and help from their families, the Dragans were able to support themselves through the leanest times.

Wildwater built its tiny business around a two-day New River trip. The excursionists put in at Prince and rafted the relatively mellow water of the

Tom Dragan: "Wildwater boats rarely touched the ground." Guides would lift them from the trailer and set them directly in the water. *Dragan Collection.*

Upper New on the first day. They took out that evening at Thurmond, where they camped. And then the next morning, they floated the warm-up rapids into the bigger, heavier water of the Lower Gorge. During the week, Wildwater ran its office out of Thurmond.

The second year they were there, Mr. Pugh asked Jon and Melanie if they were interested in buying a home. "We thought it was really a great deal, because it had all these antiques in it," said Melanie. Unfortunately, the antiques were gone when they moved in. Melanie still lives in that house.

Soon, Jon's fascination with the area's coal history made it into the trip itinerary as well. As time went on and customers began to show, Wildwater bought more boats, and the Dragans delved deeper into the abandoned towns that dotted the riversides. "We decided to make history as much a part of our raft trip as the whitewater was," said Tom. "We started naming our boats after towns and people in them." They began to require such knowledge in their guides, as well. "In order to work at

Wildwater," said Tom, "every year, you wrote a five-page, single-spaced paper on some facet of the history of the New River. Over the years, they did a lot of research. And our guides were just as much a part of the river trip as the river itself."

"Jon loved history," agreed Melanie. "We went to Williamsburg on our honeymoon! I can't tell you how many times I've been to colonial Virginia!"

Melanie and the Dragans were the first Wildwater guides, but it wasn't long before they needed help and began to seek out others. Jon was again taking college classes, this time at California State Teacher's College in Pennsylvania. He found other boaters there and convinced them to come down. "We also had a lot of weekend warriors," said Melanie. "Jon would meet people and say, 'Hey you want to be a river guide?'"

"They trained all the time. They trained in the evening when they came off the river. They did throw ropes. They did knots. We used to go through a whole week of training classes," remembered Melanie. Jon even brought in a snake expert to lecture and teach the guides to identify snakes. A rope-access expert, Bruce Smith, taught all the knots, ropes and z-drags. Jon even anchored a tire tube in the middle of the river for guides to practice with throw ropes. "If they got it right in the middle," said Melanie, "they got a beer or something. There was always some sort of incentive." Guides learned first aid and CPR, too. Wildwater hired EMTs to come and teach.

One of the first local West Virginians to become a Wildwater guide was Bob Underwood, who had spent lazy summer days as a boy floating down the New River in homemade wooden boats. "I heard they were running the New River," said Underwood. "I just said, well, I think I'll go down and talk to them, since I grew up down there. I said, 'I'd like to run the rapids with you two guys.' I explained that I grew up here, and that I knew some about the river. So, Jon said sure." Dragan told him a time and place to meet, and before he knew it, Underwood had run farther downstream than he ever had before.

Wildwater was growing quickly, so the Dragans added more boats, this time New River rafts, which, like the Green River rafts, were Rubber Fabricators creations. At twenty feet long, sporting twenty-four-inch-diameter outer tubes and four sixteen-inch-diameter cross tubes, the New River rafts were humongous. "Depending on how many people you

Wildwater guides at the Caperton House in the Caperton ghost town of the New River Gorge. Jon Dragan made sure that all his guides knew as much as possible about the cultural history of the New River. That practice continues at several raft companies today. *Butch Christian Collection.*

had and their weight," said Underwood, "it was almost like loading an aircraft. If you had a whole bunch of people that were a little overweight, you would have to distribute that weight around just so you could paddle the boat down the river."

Wildwater developed a two-guide method to muscle the behemoths downstream. The stern guide—also known as the long-range person—was responsible for looking downstream, assessing the level of the water and the rapid itself and lining the boat up far before it actually arrived at the rapid. He or she needed to set the boat's angle correctly and put it in the flow so when it entered the rapid it was in the best location relative to the current and pointed the right way. The bow guide was the short-range person. He or she moved the boat through the rapid itself. "If you were lucky enough," said Underwood, "you had two up front."

Before adding the big boats, the company was still being stymied by occasional high water, which the Dragans viewed as too dangerous to run. "Safety was a priority to Jon," said Melanie. "When the river got above five feet, we didn't run it. So he tried to figure out ways he could take people down and experience the trip." The New River rafts weighed 450 to 500 pounds. "The tubes got bigger because they figured they could run at a higher level." The new boats increased Wildwater's cutoff from five feet on the river gauge to nine.

It was only the beginning. "We tried triple rigs, which were three Green River rafts lashed together side by side, and a person sat in the middle with these two huge oars," recalled Melanie. "But what happened was, when you get in someplace like Keeney's Creek, the middle boat goes into a hole and the outer boats would buckle, and you had no control! So, we never ran commercial trips in triple rigs. The guys tried lots of methods, and that's when they came up with the pig rigs."

Pig rigs were pontooned catamaran rafts with aluminum frames strapped atop, seats and even a railing to keep people in. They also sported fifty-horsepower Mercury motors—no paddles necessary. "We did trips in the wintertime when we got those, and we were also able to walk into the old towns then because we didn't have to worry about snakes." Pig rigs could haul sixteen people. The motor did all the work.

The water level would determine how high upstream they put in with the pig rigs. When the New River was high and fast, "we would go to Prince or Sandstone or wherever, so customers got the whole day on the river," said Tom. "Sometimes we'd combine that with a trip to the expedition mine, and then Prince to Thurmond, eat lunch at Thurmond, then to Fayette Station, so when people made the effort to come, they got a full day's entertainment." Wildwater eventually had five pig rigs, which it also began to rent to other outfitters. "We only flipped one. Jeff Proctor [a principal owner of Class-VI] was in it. I think the Park Service bought one. Chris had one. I think he even still has one left."

The company even experimented with mule trips in the winter. "Jon tried all kinds of new ideas to bring people into the area. It was hard in the beginning, because people didn't know what whitewater was. Jon was always trying to find a new idea to build an industry," said Melanie. "He was always looking for ways to make things better. He was very innovative. He was the idea person."

Nick Rahall, the Democratic congressman from West Virginia, interacted with Jon often after he was elected to office and had begun to work on creating the New River Gorge National River. He remembers Dragan as "a determined individual! Very persistent. He was responsive to every question that was raised of him and not willing to take no for an answer. A dogged determination that has benefited our area untold number of times over."

There was, however, "no grand scheme, despite what some people think," said Tom. "Class VI, MRT, they might be different, they might have sat down with a business plan. We were just doing things we liked to do, and it worked out."

"We didn't have much at Thurmond base camp until the early '80s," said Tom. "I mean, it was a horse field." They kept the grass cut and hung oil-filled lanterns in front of tents, in which many of their customers slept. "And everybody just hung out and had a good time," continued Tom. "We'd get up at seven in the morning, have breakfast, do the safety orientation and put in on the river." Wildwater trips were on the river at ten minutes to 8:00 a.m. every day. They didn't take out until 4:30 p.m., sometimes 5:00 p.m.

At the time, there was no midpoint access at Cunard. "I don't care if the water was eight feet or two feet or minus two," said Tom. "You put in at Thurmond, and you beat your brains out getting down there. You swam, you paddled, you told jokes, you told history. It was as laid back and outdoorsy as you could get."

Wildwater's first commercial Gauley trip was in September 1971. Melanie remembers it well, because "we were supposed to be married the weekend of the twenty-fourth and twenty-fifth of September. Then they received word from the Corps of Engineers that they were releasing water, and I had to change my wedding date to October."

Those early Gauley Wildwater trips were also two days long but, curiously, didn't involve much camping, other than at the put-in. Trips paddled halfway down the river, and then Wildwater hauled them out, picked up guides and guests at Panther Mountain and took them back to camp at the dam. "We would literally move our base camp from Thurmond to the dam," said Melanie. "After a while, we figured what the heck, we'll just stay in a motel, and we spent a lot of time eating at Country Road Inn. That became just as much a part of our trip as the river." Guides and guests alike wined and dined all evening, and then Wildwater hauled everybody back to the river the next morning to complete the trip.

"Every day was an experience," said Tom. "There were no rules. There were no books. You could do whatever you wanted, as long as nobody got hurt."

"Unfortunately, it did evolve into a business," said Tom. "When it evolved into a business for us, that's about the time other people started to come along. And then—I'm not saying it wasn't fun—but there was

Before West Virginia built the New River Gorge Bridge, a commute to and from the Gauley River from Thurmond was a major affair. Wildwater dodged the problem by camping at the dam, circa early 1970s. *Butch Christian Collection.*

another aspect to it that we didn't necessarily buy into for whatever reason: the competition."

As new companies began to join the fray, Jon's personality, which some viewed as coarse, would again come into play. Jon would eventually find himself at the center of the New River rafting industry's biggest controversy, which revolved around Wildwater's ownership and control of Fayette Station, a convenient takeout point upstream of a grueling flat-water section called Hawk's Nest Lake. That was not, however, the only time he was at odds with others on the river.

"Jon would normally put in early," said Paul Breuer, owner and founder of the New River's second (or is it third?) rafting company, Mountain River Tours (MRT). "We'd never see him."

One day, however:

> *We had an early trip for some reason. We were on Jump Rock, and here comes Jon with eight or ten rafts and he surrounds us. We couldn't jump! Jon got on my raft and said, "That's my rock! Get off my GD rock!" I said, "I don't see any signs, and by the way, you're on my raft. Get off my raft!" And that was basically the start of our conversations for another ten years.*

Breuer remembers another Dragan story that involved his friend Bob Morgan, who is himself a major figure in New River rafting history. A Morgan trip camped at Stone Cliff, intending to put in again the next day, but overnight, the water rose to an unacceptable level, and the group had to cancel. Dragan was there that day, and Breuer left him and Morgan at Stone Cliff while he shuttled customers back to MRT's base in Hico. When he left, the two men were calmly discussing how to run the river. "I remember coming back and seeing both men standing on rocks or trailers," said Breuer, "not on the ground. One was trying to get higher than the other, arguing about how to run the river. I could hear them from a quarter mile away. It went on and on, and finally I said, 'Hey guys, I want to go home.'"

Despite his sometimes abrasive nature, Jon continued to lead Wildwater into successful currents. Neither he nor Melanie and Tom, however, were completely happy with the competitive state of the industry. "We did really well in the outfitting business, until about the early '80s," said Tom.

> *That's when I think it got competitive. Even in the late '70s, Class-VI came along, and things were going pretty good. And then all of a sudden, to me it got, not cutthroat, but it was probably more important to get people to come to your facility to take them down the river, so you could make more money, than it was to just go out and run the river.*

By 1984, the Park Service began to make offers to buy Wildwater's land so it could add the parcels to the park. "And for me," said Tom. "I was ready to get out, because I wasn't interested in competing with all the other outfitters and to cut corners just to make more money. So, we found other things to do."

In 1990, Wildwater sold three pieces of land to the National Park Service, including thirty-odd acres at Stone Cliff above Thurmond, five acres at base camp and five or six acres at Fayette Station. "We had been talking to them for about seven or eight years, telling them no, no, no," said Tom. "They finally came up with a price that was more than fair. At that point, Jon and I probably knew we were getting out of it. I had two sons and a wife, and rafting takes a lot of time for seven months out of the year. It was an easy decision for me."

After cutting the deal with the Park Service, the Dragans began to look for a buyer for the company. Jon, Melanie and Tom sold their interests in Wildwater in 1990. "Chris decided he had plenty of time left," said Tom, "and he became part of the new Wildwater." The company continued to operate out of Thurmond for two more years, before moving operations downstream to Lansing.

What Jon, Melanie and Tom left behind was a thriving industry rapidly approaching its peak and running tens of thousands of happy people down the river each year. Tom is still adamant that none of it was planned and that from his family's perspective, everything was for the most part done spontaneously. Of Jon, however, he also said, "Once he set his mind to something, he did it. It all was his idea, without a doubt."

Jon Dragan, who was larger than life, outspoken, dedicated to the history of the New River and the father of the West Virginia whitewater rafting industry as we know it, passed of stroke in February 2005 at the all-too-young age of sixty-two. I never met him, but I feel like I know him just a little, and I miss him.

Interlude

THE TURKEY RAFT

To the soundtrack of a growing roar in the chilly, soggy October air of 1969, a small raft floated ever closer to a collection of three rapids that would eventually become known on the New River as the Keeney Brothers. Jon Dragan's Wildwater Unlimited had been in operation for only year, and the New River was virtually devoid of traffic.

The little raft floated effortlessly through the first drop, Upper Keeney, but as it passed to the right of a house-sized boulder called Whale Rock, it was obvious to the crew that part two of those rapids, Middle Keeney, would not be as easy as it looked when they had scouted it from shore—and it had actually seemed quite difficult. The water was low that day, and the powerfully built, clean-cut Bob Morgan worked the oars furiously to control the boat's angle as Jim Jones and Paul Breuer paddled hard at the bow to keep the raft in the flow and off the many exposed rocks. At six feet, three inches and 240 pounds, "Big Jim" Wahlke weighed down the stern.

Their efforts were not up to the task. The boat slipped over a partially submerged rock and fell from a pour-over in midstream. It flipped instantly, dumping all four of its crew into the frigid water.

Morgan, who owned a burgeoning canoe livery business in Fort Ancient, Ohio, on the banks of the Little Miami River and who led the team, invented and oversaw the handcrafting of the boat, whose crew had christened it "the Turkey Raft," two days earlier.

To an observer today, the Turkey Raft would look curious indeed. Compared to kayaks and even canoes, today's whitewater rafts are not exactly the picture of sleekness and aqua dynamics, but this boat was in a whole other league of ugly. "We cut a piece of circular plywood, big enough that it wouldn't fit through the hole," described Breuer.

> *We ran four ropes at twelve, three, six and nine around the tube and through the floor, so we could stand inside.*
>
> *We basically got the inner tubes free. They were earth-mover, tire-sized inner tubes. Bob had old oak flooring left over. He said hey, that's strong stuff. It doesn't cost me anything, except for the horns to hold the oars. Those were made out of half-inch rod. He hinged it in the middle, which was kind of funky, how it all worked. It was based on the western design—everything was center mount.*

"It was the first self-bailing raft, I think," proclaimed Breuer, "because water just drained out. That's my claim and I'm sticking to it."

From front to back, Jim Jones, Paul Breuer, Bob Morgan and Big Jim Wahlke mere moments before capsizing in Middle Keeney on the Turkey Raft's maiden voyage in 1969. *Bob Lynn.*

Morgan, Breuer, Jones and Wahlke had arrived twenty-five miles upstream at 2:00 a.m. in a fifteen-degree morning two days prior to their flip at Middle Keeney, with four other people and another, more standard raft. Morgan's wife, June, and eleven-year-old son, Dirk, were along, as were Cincinnati journalist Bob Lynn, who was there to chronicle the expedition, and his wife, Millie, and Don MeDert, who worked for the Morgans in Ohio.

Lynn later wrote that Morgan led the expedition,

> *following a dream: to offer people in the East whitewater rafting—à la Colorado River rafting so popular in the West.*
>
> *A man who for eleven summers has taken boys on canoe trips on whitewater rivers in Canada, Kentucky, Tennessee and West Virginia, Morgan wanted to know if rafts could traverse the New River's famous Lower Gorge.*

The small flotilla started near the town of Prince, West Virginia, so they would have many miles of relatively unchallenging water in which to familiarize themselves with their boats. Before setting off that first morning, Dirk found a collection of wild turkey feathers, "and—presto," wrote Lynn, "our craft was dubbed the 'Turkey Raft'—ugly, but game as hell."

Lynn and the Morgans rode the Turkey Raft, while Breuer, Jones and Wahlke rode a more conventional model. MeDert's role was to ferry camp supplies along the road and run shuttle.

They had minor doubts about the Turkey Raft's ability to navigate the exposed rocks in the current. "The water was really low," said Breuer. "And Bob Lynn said, 'This is crazy. This is the lowest I've ever seen this river.'"

Lynn, a reporter for the *Enquirer* magazine in Cincinnati called the Army Corps of Engineers, which controlled the Bluestone Dam, to find out why the water was so low. "They said, 'There's a fishing study, and we're testing the fishability of different flows,'" said Breuer. "Bob said, 'Oh, you can't do that! We're doing this rafting trip and blah, blah, blah. We want more water.' I think that was the first request for more water. We didn't get it, of course. It was about 870 cfs."

Nevertheless, the group set out. "Morgan's booming voice, echoing off the mountain sides with the clarity of hammer to anvil," wrote Lynn,

> *became a familiar sound above the roar of the rapids. 'Ferry left…back paddle, everybody back paddle…watch that rock…forward, forward, forward…ferry right…that's it…beautiful, just great.'*
>
> *And as we bobbed successfully into calm water, a wall-to-wall grin spread across Morgan's handsome, youthful face. The turkey raft was proving to be amazingly maneuverable and capable.*

The team knew, however, that the most difficult rapids of the Lower Gorge lay ahead. They ended their second day on the water at the town of Thurmond, and MeDert shuttled everybody to Fayette Station, where they made camp. The next day, Morgan, Breuer, Jones and Lynn piled back into the Turkey Raft at Thurmond to have at it. Wahlke hiked alongside the river and scouted the rapids from shore, and the rest of team waited at camp downstream for the little boat to arrive.

"As we bobbed down the river," wrote Lynn, "the waving party on shore grew dim in the drizzling overcast."

Melanie Dragan also recalls the Turkey Raft. "It was funny, because when they'd get to the major rapids, they would wait until we ran first, and then come through. We'd stop for lunch, and they'd stop. You'd look out there and see these rafts stacked up on a frame. They looked like Tom Sawyer."

Above the Keeney Brothers rapids, Wahlke and Lynn traded places because Lynn wanted to shoot movie film from shore. It was a choice Wahlke would regret, as mere minutes later Morgan and crew were in the icy water at Middle Keeney.

Lynn described what he saw through his camera lens:

> *In one horrifying instant, I saw Morgan, Jones, Breuer and Wahlke spilling into the water as the raft turned completely over on top of them…I got a jerky strip of, first Morgan, then Wahlke being swept down through the rapids…The raft was torn apart, one tube already having been swept away. The other was hung up on another rock with the framework. Perched like crawldads* [sic] *on top of the inner tube were Jones and Breuer…Breuer, a gangling six-foot-five-incher, reached into the water and cut the tube from the wood frame. Hanging on for dear life, away they went, spinning and pitching crazily down through the frothing rapids.*

> *Once in the lower pool, they were almost swept into the next rapids (ones twice as dangerous), but by staying with the tube, finally made safely to the opposite shore.*

The group later came back with a modified Turkey Raft and was successful; in 1970, Morgan and Breuer also made attempts on the Upper Gauley and Lower Meadow Rivers in half Turkey Rafts—one tube and no frame. Neither of those trips was successful, but Breuer was in love with these rivers.

In May 1970, Lynn's article on the maiden voyage of the Turkey Raft appeared in the *Enquirer* magazine. "Wild Trip Down Wild River" eventually led to the first boom in commercial whitewater rafting on the New River, as requests for such experiences flooded into Morgan's canoe livery in Ohio. Though Morgan himself was too wrapped up in his booming canoe business and in raising his young family to participate directly, he sold Paul Breuer and Paul's partners the rafts upon which they floated the foundation of the second raft company in the New River Gorge—Mountain River Tours.

Or were they the third?

THE RISE OF THE OUTFITTERS

In 1970, Wildwater was still the only game in town, and the Dragans basked in the glow of solitude from their isolated base camp in Thurmond. People were already calling West Virginia whitewater rafting an "industry," but how much of an industry can you have with only one company?

"There were like four outfitters on the Yough and us down here," said Tom. "I'm sure there were others, but it was so small scale. It just wasn't a big deal."

It was not to be that way for long. Two more companies would rise quickly from obscurity, but which of them can rightly claim the title of second is at issue, especially to their founders.

Without making any claim that Mountain River Tours (MRT) was the undeniable second company to take paying customers down the New River, let's start there.

Together with his business partners, Paul Breuer (of Turkey Raft fame) incorporated MRT in 1973, but "we actually ran two years before that. I did it just in summer with a guy named Rick Wry and another guy," said Breuer. The three of them brought people down on weekends from Ohio to raft the New River. "I think we did maybe six trips or something."

"We came down here and basically bootstrapped it," he continued. "None of us had much money. In fact, I had none. Mine was sweat equity. I didn't want to sit behind a desk or be tied down or anything else. It was incredibly difficult—where's your next dollar coming from? How can you get food? I was living in an old garage in Hico for the first year…that's how we ran the business."

Breuer moved to the region full time in 1973 to put all his effort into MRT. The company's first customers came from the Cincinnati area and Bob Morgan's Fort Ancient canoe livery. Bob Lynn's article in the *Enquirer* about the Turkey Raft expedition stirred up no small amount of interest there and resulted in what Breuer described as thousands of requests to Morgan for raft trips in West Virginia.

Soon, MRT was running large numbers on the New River and a growing base on the Gauley as well. But Gauley access was spread wide. Rafts could put in at the dam and take out at the town of Swiss, twenty-six miles downstream, which made for a long day. If boaters wanted to split up the trip, they needed to camp or brave a long, steep walk out at Panther Mountain. Breuer was the first to develop

Wildwater guide Roy Hugh Barrett guides from the bow on Upper Railroad, Lower New River, circa 1971. *Dragan Collection.*

midpoint access on the Gauley, when MRT purchased property on river left at Wood's Ferry. It is difficult to find anybody, in fact, who doesn't credit Paul Breuer with developing the rafting industry as a whole on the Gauley.

For MRT, the future began to brighten significantly in the mid-1970s. "It was '76, probably '77, when we were looking at expanding," said Breuer. An acquaintance of his, Michael Tousey, who worked as an attorney for the Sierra Club, also wanted to get involved. "He moved to North Carolina at the French Broad River. That's when we started up Carolina Wilderness Adventures. Then we went over to Kentucky and had Cumberland Outdoor Adventures for a number of years."

Breuer and his good friend Imre Szilagyi (pronounced IM-ruh sill-AH-jee), who founded Appalachian Wildwaters about the same time MRT formed, argue often, politely but vehemently, about which man's company plied the rivers of West Virginia for money first. "I was first," said Breuer. "He says other things, but boil it down to Department of Natural Resources license number. He won't go there!"

"That's absolutely a phony argument," countered Szilagyi in his deep voice and Hungarian accent. "It's just the first year they were giving permits," which didn't occur until 1979. "It's just in the order in which you applied. He's full of shit. There was nobody on the rivers except Ralph McCarty on the Cheat and Jon Dragan on the New, and there was no sign of Paul Breuer. I think the record is clear."

"I can prove that I took something down that was commercial, no bones about it, in 1972," continued Szilagyi. "He didn't even own any rafts in 1972."

In 1970 and 1971, Szilagyi, a mathematician by both vocation and avocation, also worked as a raft guide on the Lower Yough. "I followed some lady into whitewater in about 1970, and the lady left, but the whitewater stayed." Szilagyi then began guiding to support his whitewater habit. The deal netted him twenty dollars for a day's work, plus a free lunch and shuttle. Gas was twenty-five cents a gallon, "and that covered my gas money and provided me an audience for showing off."

He guided rafts, however, from a kayak. The approach, called "self-guiding," was common on the Yough. "You put a guide in the first raft to make sure nobody passed you," explained Szilagyi, "and a guide in the last raft to make sure everybody was in front of you, and then you had two kayakers that picked up pieces. We were basically sheep dogs, making sure people didn't get stuck."

"On Class-III or lesser water, the raft guide was a herder. On Class-IV-plus water, the guide was muscle. He was a hero and a river god. The customer was 'cargo,' 'carp' or a 'touron.'"

Though Appalachian Wildwaters (AW) took its first commercial trip on the New River in 1972, at the time, customers were few and far between. "You could probably count them on one hand," laughed Szilagyi.

To Szilagyi, the problems with self-guided rafts were numerous and obvious, and he founded AW with a more customer-centric approach to guiding. He had experience teaching mathematics as a graduate student at Ohio State University, and he noticed then that new students weren't learning well with older, outdated teaching methods:

> *When you teach a mathematician, you give him the facts and let him figure it out, and a whole lot of the Ohio State students, you couldn't do that. Instead of calling them names, you had to try it differently. This is a huge problem at large land-grant universities; how do you teach non-mathematicians enough mathematics so they can function effectively, so they can use statistics with some integrity.*

Szilagyi and his co-teachers examined what they felt were the reasons why their students had such a difficult time grasping calculus. "We found that by not screaming at them and calling them bloody idiots that they would eventually perform."

This became one of the keys to AW's guiding approach. "I think we changed what guiding was about," he said.

> *We looked at the guide as a coach, as a teacher and a psychologist and a social worker. The question was, could the customer be relied on at critical points? Particularly at Whale Rock, would they freak out on you and push you into losing control at Middle Keeney? Or at Double Z, when you made the turn behind Devil's Tooth, would they screw up your run and push you into the undercut at bottom left?*

Szilagyi thought that with his approach to guiding, it wouldn't be an issue. Today, that approach is not just common on the Lower New and Gauley Rivers, it's the norm.

"We trained and taught the customers how to react appropriately," he said. "If somebody was afraid, you worked them through their concerns. The customer was a participant, and he was part of the crew."

The bonus in the equation was that changing the relationship between the customer and the guide also changed the relationship between the customer and the company. To AW's customers, it was obvious that the company valued them as people and relied on them to perform. It brought about a mutual respect, and AW's customer count soared.

"I think the guide who saw himself as a river god had contempt for the customer," mused Szilagyi, "And the only thing that covered up that contempt was an attempt to suck a tip out of them." By 1985, AW

Butch Christian and crew plow into Surprise, circa mid-1970s. Unseen in this photo: most of an eighteen-foot-long raft and at least eight other people. *Butch Christian Collection.*

was the largest river outfitter in West Virginia—50 percent larger than number two, which was North American River Runners.

However, also in 1985, factors beyond Szilagyi's control conspired to knock his company from its perch.

In founding Appalachian Wildwaters, Szilagyi initiated a business model that included three rivers. They ran the Cheat River in the spring, the New River in the summer and the Gauley River whenever the Corps of Engineers, which controlled flows at the Summersville Dam, had scheduled drawdowns of Summersville Lake. They executed that plan successfully and with single-minded focus until, on November 5, 1985, torrential rains sent an immense flood roaring through the Cheat Valley. "We experienced massive damage," Szilagyi lamented. "We lived on the Cheat. All of our equipment was stored in our outpost and got carried down river."

Overnight, AW went from running eighteen thousand customers on the Cheat, New and Gauley Rivers combined to being incapable of taking any at all.

"Our documented replacement cost was, I believe, three times our net worth," said Szilagyi.

Much like Jon Dragan, Imre Szilagyi has a reputation for occasional gruffness but also for intelligence and determination to succeed where others might not. After losing everything in a day, anybody else would have hung it up, tossed in the towel, rolled over and died. He did the exact opposite. "The only way I thought we could remain competitive was to grow very rapidly, and that's when we bought out companies in Tennessee and North Carolina, on the Tygart [in West Virginia] and in Texas."

His actions saved Appalachian Wildwaters, but it also spread the company thin geographically. AW would never be number one in West Virginia again. "My story is that I got distracted in Tennessee and North Carolina, and Class-VI and ACE passed me," he laughed.

The 1985 flood decimated more than just AW's operation. It essentially spelled the near demise of commercial whitewater rafting on the Cheat River in general. Over the course of the next ten years, the industry on the Cheat lost around 10 percent of its business every year. "In 1985, the industry took down over thirty thousand customers," explained Szilagyi. By the turn of the millennium, "I doubt we took down more than a couple thousand."

Long before floodwaters erased AW's operation on the Cheat River, a fourth outfitter (and several others, for that matter) sprang from MRT's loins in an infamous and tumultuous 1977 event that old-timers affectionately call "The Guide Strike."

Dave Arnold, one of the principal owners of Class-VI and now Adventures on the Gorge, was an MRT guide when the Guide Strike went down. He looks back at it as a tipping point. "No question, the Guide Strike started four or five companies: Drift-a-Bit with Randall Ballard, New & Gauley Expeditions with Keith Spangler, Class-VI and even some other ones, like Beauty Mountain. We went from three outfitters—MRT, AW and Wildwater—to a bunch of outfitters real quickly."

He is, however, very careful to point out that the Guide Strike was not actually a strike, per se. "Even though it's called the 'Guide Strike,' for history's sake, there was never a strike. There was never a work closure." That perspective contrasts starkly with the legend of the strike, which, if it is to be believed, shut down the entire industry for a month.

The strike began as not much more than a joke among MRT guides, who were putting in hard hours for Paul Breuer and crew. "To put it into context," explained Arnold, "we put in at Thurmond every day. It didn't matter if the river was running nine hundred cfs, and we went all the way to Hawk's Nest, sometimes with a boat tow." Going all the way to Hawk's Nest involves a stretch of the New River called Hawk's Nest Lake, a four-mile expanse of flat water, which is the rafting equivalent of carrying a loaded boat up four miles of thirty-degree uphill slope. "Some of us lived in Oak Hill," he continued, "and this was pre-bridge." MRT guides had to leave Oak Hill, wind their way down Route 82 past Fayette Station, cross the little bridge at the bottom of the New River Gorge, go to work in Hico (a few miles north of the gorge) and check in with their guests. On a bus with guests, they then had to wend down Route 60 to Hawk's Nest Park, climb around Cotton Hill and drive to Thurmond, where they put in fourteen miles upstream. Then they rafted to Hawk's Nest, including four miles of lake, and hopped on a bus from Hawk's Nest back to base at Hico. Once they waved goodbye to their guests, they still had to reverse the morning commute to get back home.

"It was insanity!" said Arnold.

Breuer's guides asked him for ten dollars more per day. "We were working a lot of days, and if my memory is right, we were making seventeen dollars a day," said Arnold.

"I remember eighteen dollars," said Doug Proctor, another former MRT guide and current principal player in Adventures on the Gorge.

"We didn't really think we were asking for that much," Arnold added.

The movement started approximately three weeks prior to the Fourth of July weekend, when MRT had three full days scheduled. "There was just a lot of bitching about not making enough money," said Arnold. "Somebody said, 'We need to form the United Brotherhood of Whitewater Workers.' We actually had a T-shirt: UBWW. There were crossed oars on them. We were just being goofballs as much as anything, and then it started to take on some seriousness."

MRT guides told management that if they would not comply with their request for more money, they would not work on the Fourth of July weekend. "But we never walked out," said Arnold, his finger in the air. "I consider it more of a negotiation."

"I'm sure it was also very tough on the owners," he added. "Paul was fairly willing to listen, and Mike Marine and Mike Tousey, being outside businesspeople, took it, in my opinion, too seriously." Breuer's partners weren't on site and didn't know the guides, and that gap between their perspectives turned the situation from something that nobody took to be entirely dire into something quite serious.

While Arnold and Jeff Proctor, Doug's brother and now also a principal in Adventures on the Gorge, maintain that the legend of the Guide Strike is overblown, Breuer, himself now high in the Adventures on the Gorge chain of command, views it as a low point in his career as a raft company owner. "It was like two cars coming at each other head on, and who's going to chicken out first?" he said.

"I thought the wages were fair for that time," he continued. "There were some longer days, and maybe there was some need for an increase." No doubt, the company was growing rapidly at the time as well. In 1977, it was running 250 customers downstream a day, which was unheard of.

Breuer is quick to take responsibility for the role he played; perhaps too much so. "It was partially my fault in not communicating well enough with the staff. Maybe I hadn't matured enough as a manager to sit them down and say, okay, let's talk. I rarely got on the river then, except to train, and that wasn't good."

One guide in particular, whose name nobody seems to remember, was the most vocal. "He just came up one day, it was July Fourth weekend, and said we want a ten-dollar raise per day. There was no way."

"Well," the guide scolded Breuer, "then we're not working." He told Breuer that he and the rest of the guides would be at the garage if he wanted to come and talk.

"They were over there having a big party," said Breuer.

He discussed the situation with his partners, but it was clear the financials of a ten-dollar raise wouldn't work out. "We made them an offer of a couple dollars," recalled Breuer, but they turned him down flatly.

"I asked, who's in this? And they claimed everybody was," said Breuer. It turned out, however, that most of the part-time guides had no inkling what was happening.

MRT was booked solid for three days and looking down the barrel of a loaded financial loss. "I didn't get any sleep that night," said Breuer, who talked back and forth with the partners. "About one or two in the morning, I was so frustrated. I saw the company as my whole life going down, and these guys weren't being reasonable. I couldn't negotiate with them."

When the next morning dawned, Breuer made a final proposal of five dollars more per day, "and they said, 'Yeah, we'll do that!'"

And then the part-time guides showed up for work. Breuer shook his head as he recalled the morning. "They said, really? We're getting a five-dollar raise? No way! How did that happen? I was like, what? You guys didn't know about this?"

"I was just a first-year guide," agreed Doug Proctor. "I just walked in on it. I didn't care. I just wanted to guide."

"Still, sometimes," said Breuer, "I have to look back at it as a learning experience."

Though they recall talking about starting their own company prior to that weekend, there's no doubt that the strike was a milestone in the inception of Class-VI River Runners. None of the strike leaders, including Arnold and Jeff Proctor, were invited back the next season. "I got a letter that said, 'Hey, we heard your brother and Dave and them are starting their own company,'" said Doug, "'but if you want to come back with us, feel free to.' They didn't know I was part of it."

By October, Arnold, the Proctors and another guide named Kevin "Catfish" Whelan were looking for land. By November, they were working with somebody on their brochure. "We were in motion," said Arnold. "I think we incorporated in December."

"You gotta put yourself back in that time period," Arnold continued. He and Jeff Proctor had taught kayaking in North Carolina and had worked with Breuer and Bob Morgan once before in Canada, so they had knowledge of river current and how to propel a boat down it. It was knowledge few others had. Breuer and the Dragans had started to introduce these concepts to local people and train them on how to run a river, but those people were still the minority.

Wildwater rafts run Miller's Folly on the Lower New River, circa 1971. Note the French-made Flother Chok life jacket, which was not Coast Guard approved, on the men at left. *Tom Evans, West Virginia Department of Commerce Collection.*

"There were no restrictions," Arnold said, as he shook his head. "There were no closed permits. The only thing to stop you from getting a license was twenty-five dollars."

Soon enough, however, "the state recognized that it could be five hundred outfitters if they didn't do something," said Arnold. Concerned about the carrying capacity of the New and Gauley Rivers, and that numbers were growing too rapidly and were apt to get out of control, the West Virginia Department of Natural Resources (DNR) began to refuse to grant new licenses.

Records are spotty at best in explaining precisely when this occurred, and outfitters' memories equally so. What appears to be the case is that the West Virginia state legislature granted the DNR's Whitewater Commission power to control licenses in 1981 and to limit the numbers of customers any one outfitter could carry down the rivers on any given day. In 1999, the legislature made the moratorium on new licenses the law of the land.

According to records held by the West Virginia Professional River Outfitters Association (WVPRO), there are currently twenty-six licenses in existence, which seven companies now own between themselves. Arnold recalls the number of licenses being somewhere closer to thirty-seven at its peak, but some of those may only have been valid on the Cheat River, and it's not inconceivable that some of them also dissolved when the companies that owned them folded. The state's records are likewise unclear on the subject.

Licenses are like gold now to the industry. It is unlikely that any more of them will either appear or disappear. Even if another company folds, a larger company is likely to purchase its license. Indeed, when one raft company purchases another, items like permits and equipment are usually the deal's prime fodder. Other assets, such as land, are often left out of the equation entirely.

Together with existing outfitters, the Whitewater Commission also created a degree of parity among licenses. Larger permits stayed the same, but smaller units, which once had various numbers from as low as 40 attached to them, enlarged dramatically. A license, for example, that was previously worth 40 people per day on the New River became worth 120 overnight. Parity gave companies that owned multiple licenses free reign to grow precisely when the industry was experiencing its most rapid spurt—and it ensured that no new competitors could join the fray. For those fortunate companies, it was like adding oxygen to a fire. Other companies that, for example, owned one permit that was already good for 112 people only saw an 8-person-per-day increase. For them, it was like sucking the air out of the room.

Understandably, as outfitters, bureaucrats and politicians wrangled over license allocations, disagreements ensued. Present and former outfitters still sometimes refer to that time as the allocation wars.

"I think Keith Spangler [of New & Gauley Expeditions] got the last permit," said Arnold. "Outfitters, guides, legislators…a bunch of people realized that if we didn't do something, the river could be too crowded. The business model could fall apart. You only have to look at the Arkansas River to see it. At one point, the Arkansas had eighty permits or something."

One company that would go on to make a huge mark on the industry was ACE Raft, which incorporated in 1979. ACE's name is an acronym that stands for American Canadian Expeditions. Strangely enough, the acronym came first, and its owners decided later what it stood for. They chose "ACE" for the sole reason that it would appear first in the phone book. "That's one of the best things we ever did," said Ernie Kincaid, one of ACE's principal owners. They chose American Canadian, because, originally, they fully intended to also run trips on the Ottawa River in Ontario. They never did paddle a stroke in Canada, but the name worked for them, and they kept it.

Kincaid was born down the road from Oak Hill and is one of the few remaining "local" raft company owners. "I moved here when I was born," he laughed, "down in Page-Kincaid area."

In 1969, Kincaid and two friends were driving along in Fayette County, which even then was becoming a hotbed of whitewater activity, when one of them said, "Let's get canoes!"

"I went home and told my mom, and she said, 'The guy I work for has some kayaks in his office.' I ended up getting a C1."

Kincaid paddled hard boats often and only guided rafts a handful of times before starting ACE. "I guided twice for Rivermen…when they begged," he laughed. "But I was never really a guide."

Then, in late 1979, Kincaid jumped into the fray with both feet. He purchased four used boats from Wildwater and then quickly realized that he needed paddles, too. "You have to have helmets," he rambled. "You have to have trailers to haul it all and trucks to pull them. And then you have to have insurance. The more stuff you buy, the more people you have to haul to support it. The more people you haul, the more stuff you have to buy. It's never-ending."

ACE started out as just Ernie Kincaid and a partner, Doug McKenzie, sharing the load 50-50. The pair bought an old school bus at auction, which didn't actually run. "I had it up at the local garage," recalled Kincaid, who worked as a mining engineer in Nicholas County, the office of which was just uphill from the Gauley River.

The bus sat idly in the garage for several months, until finally ACE's first trip was scheduled for the next weekend. The mechanic at the garage told Kincaid, "I can get the motor back in it, but I can't get it bolted up for you. But, I'll leave an extension cord for you to use out the bottom of the door."

Kincaid grabbed a friend, who was a mechanic, and headed for the garage. "We got the motor all bolted up. It was like three in the morning when we finally got it done. We had everything ready to go—and it wouldn't start!" After much hemming and hawing, his friend determined that the culprit was the bus's distributor coil.

"I ran down over the hill to the coal company," said Kincaid, "and stole a coil off one of the company trucks in the parking lot. I took it back over, and the bus fired right up." A few hours later, Kincaid was hauling guests to the New River in a bus with stolen parts. "That was the first ACE trip ever," he said.

That's not the only bizarre story centered on raft and guest transportation. Raft buses in general once tended to be heaps of rusting metal and cobbled-together parts. Many of the earliest weren't buses at all but gigantic dually trucks with a bed in the back covered by Conestoga wagon–style hoops and a tarp. Wildwater hauled guests around on benches in the back of such a truck.

Pretty quickly, however, nearly every company bought one or more old school buses at auction. Michael Ivey began working as a raft guide in 1980 for a small company called Drift-a-Bit. "You started out in this industry in a bus that you might have helped paint from a yellow school

A Wildwater raft runs Lower Railroad, Lower New River, circa 1971. Those who have been here recently may notice differences. This is prior to the rock at river left breaking off to choke the bottom of the channel. *Dragan Collection.*

bus to another color," said Ivey. The chances were excellent that bus had gone to auction because some Ohio school system decided it wasn't safe on surface streets anymore. That bus then spent a whole other bus lifetime on the most treacherous roads imaginable, with hairpin turns and cliffs; sometimes they were half washed away dirt roads. "I always knew that was going to be the end of me," said Ivey. "I paid special attention in first aid class and CPR because I knew there was going to be a massive bus wreck. We all had that hanging over our heads."

When talking about how far the whitewater rafting industry has come, Dave Arnold is quick to admit:

> *I'm not sure we were as smart as I like to think we were. It wasn't as orchestrated as it seems.*
>
> *There were some people who got permits who didn't have a clue what they were doing. They weren't whitewater people. They weren't businesspeople.*

> *If the plan was to create a business that grew into something that was good for West Virginia—great tax base, jobs—those kind of companies never work out. Now, sometimes these little start ups out of garages can turn into Microsoft, too, so it's a balancing act.*
>
> *When I look back, though, it worked really well. Just enough outfitters to create competition for the consumer, but not so many that it created chaos and anarchy in the industry.*

"Outfitters in West Virginia sort of smile," concluded Arnold, "because the state has done a really good job of helping the industry grow. They regulated but weren't stifling. That's not the norm."

THE BOATS

Though Bob Morgan's Turkey Raft was largely an evolutionary dead-end in and of itself, the Frankensteinian little boat was actually ahead of its time. In his quest to build a functional, inexpensive raft, he didn't just peg two innovations that would eventually change the face of whitewater rafting on the New and Gauley Rivers. He *nailed* them.

Morgan installed stern-mounted oars on his second Turkey Raft, which was a distinct departure from the western-style center mounts he used to push the first funny little boat down the Lower New River. Center-mounted oars make rafts more maneuverable by nature of simple physics—the pivot point is in the middle of the boat. Morgan, however, was seeking other advantages. Of the Turkey Raft's first attempt on the Lower New River, Bob Morgan said, "I'm a canoer; I like people to paddle. Why can't we have people paddle?"

It was to make space for those paddlers that Morgan moved his oars back. "That's really where we developed the stern-mounted oar frame with people paddling in front," explained Paul Breuer. "When he bought the old army-surplus bridge rafts, he put the frame on the rear. He wanted people to participate and paddle."

Those bridge rafts weighed a ton. "They were vulcanized," said Breuer, "and the seams were double. They were just incredibly heavy, but bombproof."

When Breuer and other Morgan disciples opened Mountain River Tours, they brought that same stern-mount concept with them, and the technique quickly caught on in commercial West Virginia rafting. Of course, the vast majority of rafts on the New and Gauley Rivers today are pure paddle rafts with no oar rigs at all. Many former MRT guides, however, still prefer a stern-mounted rig as a hybrid that gives them more direct influence over the boat's speed and angle but still involves others in the raft as more than just ballast.

"That ten-foot oar equals about three or four Norse paddles," explained Doug Proctor. "So do you think you've got a lot more control?"

"The industry here was maybe 50 percent oars," he continued. "Us, New River Scenic, Whitewater Information, Mountain River Tours, New & Gauley Expeditions, we were all running oars. And AW, Wildwater and NARR were all running paddle boats."

"It somewhat defies science," said Dave Arnold. "Meaning, oars are a great way to run a boat, but because there were more people running paddle boats than oar boats, there was more marketing that said people who run oar boats are weenies and wimps, and the only way to really do it is a paddle boat."

Perhaps marketing that shames people into doing something that might be more dangerous than the alternative simply works. Perhaps paddle boat companies were running more guests down rivers than companies that used oar rigs and could talk the technique up to more people. Whatever the reason, the paddle boat momentum became a ground swell. Potential and returning customers began to view oar rigs as a sort of carnival attraction, during which the guide did all the real work and they were just along for the ride.

It soon became obvious to Class-VI that there was a war of opinion being waged and that oar boats were losing badly. "In '87, we documented five or six hundred people that *did not run with us*," explained Proctor, "because we didn't run paddle boats."

But the companies that were responsible for such marketing and had already adopted a paddle raft program felt there was more to the equation than just opinions. "You give me a set of oars and I don't give a shit what the customers want to do, I know where the boat is going," said Imre Szilagyi. Paddles created a difference in the relationship between the raft guide and the customer, and if the rafting company knew what it was doing, it inherited the benefit of that relationship. "If you put a set of oars on a boat, the focus of the trip is on the raft guide. Take away the oars and make the raft guide coach, then the focus becomes the customers. That's what we did," said Imre, "and it took Class-VI and Paul and Keith a good long time to figure that out."

"Every night when I lay me down to bed," he continued, "I knelt down and thanked god that Class-VI was still using oars."

While oar rigs were arguably safer, it certainly wasn't true that paddle boats were inherently unsafe. Companies that used oars listened to their constituents, and slowly but surely, the industry drifted toward paddle boats.

Mob Morgan hiking out with the remains of the first Turkey Raft after its catastrophic flip in Middle Keeney, 1969. *Bob Lynn.*

The shift angered no small number of guides. "We said to our staff in '88, this year you have to go half and half, and we actually lost a couple guides," said Proctor.

Oars…paddles…it's all academic now because the battle is well and truly over, and paddles trounced oars.

The Morgan innovation that is most intriguing to raft nerds, however, has nothing to do with locomotion. It is the self-bailing boat.

With the possible exception of some catarafts, every inflatable on every river in America in the 1970s was non-self-bailing. It would be a long time before modern self-bailing rafts became an everyday sight on the New and Gauley Rivers, so it's unlikely that the Turkey Raft is their direct precursor. It is, however, undeniable that Bob Morgan—perhaps unintentionally—made a leap in whitewater technology that West Virginia raft companies would not make again for nearly twenty years.

The first company to recognize the inherent superiority of the self-bailer was ACE Raft. In 1986, ACE leapt ahead of its competition by switching its fleet to all self-bailing boats. It did so by proclaiming loudly and clearly, on the river, that self-bailers were not just safe but also inherently superior to their older brethren. "We painted 'SELF-BAILING' on the side of each raft," recalled Ernie Kincaid, "so we're going down the river and all the customers from other companies are going, 'What does self bailing mean?' They're over there with a five-gallon bucket dipping it out, and our people are relaxing, having a good time. We grew dramatically due to those rafts."

Rivermen was not far behind ACE. After somebody vandalized its entire fleet of boats in 1990, other outfitters joined together to loan it boats to finish the season, and it used its insurance money to upgrade to self-bailing boats.

Despite a new colorful nickname—"bucket boats"—non-self-bailers did not go quietly into the night. Old school rafters, especially those who plied western rivers, like the Colorado, resisted mightily. "They were saying, 'Self-bailers are dangerous. They flip too easily. They can't come out of a hole,'" said Dave Arnold. "You get stuck in a big hole with a bucket boat, they fill up, they get weight and they wash out." Traditionalists wrote entire articles about how unsafe self-bailers were. Now, of course, every commercial outfitter in West Virginia runs them 100 percent of the time.

"One of the first times I had access to a self-bailer was on a Grand Canyon trip…and I didn't take it," Arnold continued. "At the put-in we had a couple self-bailers and some bucket boats, and I didn't want one. I thought, I'll flip. I don't want to flip. It's cold! Halfway down the canyon, I'm bailing water and watching whoever it was in the self-bailer, thinking, 'Oh, my God, I'm so stupid.' That's when the light bulb went off in my head."

The first time Arnold ever ran in a self-bailer was on the Upper Gauley River, "and I can still to this day remember realizing how sloppy I could be and get away with it! I remember both Insignificant and Lost Paddle with a self-bailer and being almost giggly."

Lost Paddle is the longest rapid on the Gauley River. In fact, it's so long that people mostly think of it as multiple rapids stacked up on top of one another. First Drop is fairly straightforward, but the waves are big—certainly big enough to add significant water weight to a bucket boat. One wave at Second Drop, also known as Hawaii Five-O, makes those waves seem like ripples in a puddle. If a bucket boat wasn't completely filled by the time it got through with Hawaii Five-O, it certainly was after Third Drop. "When you ran Third Drop in Lost Paddle in a bucket boat and you're heading toward Tumble Home, and you stand up and the water in your boat is up to your throat, that was a scary moment," explained Arnold. But in a self-bailer, "you could get into the lunch cooler and get a sandwich before you hit Tumble Home. You had all the time in the world!"

Today, less-than-fond memories of bucket boats abound throughout the industry. "The old Green River rafts," remembers Tom Dragan about *One Paw* and *Two Paw*, "the floors weren't attached to the cross tubes, so when you filled up, you had two to three thousand gallons of water to bail. You could swim underneath the cross tubes."

"It was very exciting when something went wrong," said Bob Underwood. Bucket boats rarely flipped because, filled with water, they're heavy and stable, to say the least. However, "if you got one of those things wrapped around a rock, which occasionally happened, you had ten people in the water," continued Underwood. "We carried a lot of rope and pulleys. Occasionally, we had one go all the way over. That was bad news. Once you had them completely over, there was a good possibility that somebody was going to be under it."

"Here's the bottom line: no question it's a better mouse trap," declared Arnold about self-bailing rafts. "Nobody with any brains would argue any differently. I can't *imagine* somebody arguing it."

As had happened with paddle boats and oar rigs, what the public wanted, the public got. "People said, I'm not running with you unless I'm in a self-bailer," said Proctor. "We were adding self-bailers each year, little bit by little bit. Then in '91, we said, 'Let's just convert this year.' We bought $150,000 in boats that one year and became all self-bailing. Once people had that taste, they didn't want to go back to a bucket boat."

PROTECTED WATER

The history of how the New River Gorge became a National River is both long and complicated, but thankfully, it is already well documented by the National Park Service in its *New River Gorge National River Administrative History*. What follows is an abridged version.

The story, which contains far more wrangling of politicians and activists in meeting halls and Congress than it does whitewater, is as long as the river itself and begins as far back in time. The parts of it that concern whitewater rafting in the New River Gorge, however, probably began in 1962.

In that year, Appalachian Electric Power (AEP) applied to the Federal Power Commission (FPC) for a preliminary permit to study the feasibility of building a dam on the New River at the Virginia–North Carolina border. In 1965, with the study concluded, the FPC granted AEP a permit to build a two-dam hydroelectric and pumped storage facility there. Residents in and around the immediate vicinity felt that such a project represented progress and raised little objection to it. What little opposition appeared was largely ignored until 1966, when the Department of the Interior (DOI) jumped into the fray. Charged at the time with cleaning up the nation's waterways, the DOI felt that such a facility's storage capacity would not allow it to augment flows downstream to dilute chemicals spilled into the Kanawha River, of which the New River is a tributary. The DOI won its argument in FPC hearings, but instead of shutting the project down, the ruling spurred AEP on to double the size of its planned facility.

The size of the project alarmed North Carolina residents, who leapt into action to fight it. Authors of arguments, studies and political ploys jockeyed for position for years against the authors of arguments to the contrary, conflicting studies and counter ploys. The West Virginia Highlands Conservancy jumped in to lend its support against the project in 1969, and finally, in 1970, residents of Raleigh, Fayette and Summers Counties, through which the New River Gorge slices, sat up and took notice. Lifelong New River Valley residents argued that the project upstream would forever alter their beloved river, and the owner of a fledgling whitewater rafting company, Jon Dragan, felt it would destroy the business he was trying to build.

Opponents of the project saw an opening. In 1968, Congress had passed the Wild and Scenic Rivers Act. What if, they reasoned, they could win federal protection for the New River under that act? Those efforts faltered at first, until, in 1974, Senators Sam Ervin and Jesse Helms of North Carolina managed to introduce a study on the feasibility of adding the New River to the Wild and Scenic River System.

Support from many surprising parties swelled, including nearly every concerned party in West Virginia, and finally, the governor of North Carolina applied directly to the DOI for Wild and Scenic status. Secretary of the Interior Thomas Kleppe granted it for a large section of the New River in North Carolina in 1976, but the battle there was not over.

A court of appeals quickly stayed that determination and granted the FPC permission to continue with the AEP project. The decision was a slap in the face to the project's opponents, but it also jolted them into further action. CBS, ABC and NBC all reported on the battle, and the New River became a national-level issue. Environmentalists invited members of Congress on canoe trips on the river, and simple farmers became lobbyists. As 1975 rolled into 1976, more than one hundred newspapers across the country had written editorials in opposition to the project. The federal government could no longer ignore the immensity of opposition. Both the House and Senate passed bills to declare the North Carolina section of the New River Wild and Scenic, and finally, on September 1976, President Ford signed it into law.

West Virginia's New River, however, was still largely unprotected. Spurred on by the success in North Carolina, West Virginia citizens and politicians redoubled their efforts. Not content with Wild and Scenic status, they decided that a National Park was more appropriate. With support from all quarters, including the state government, citizenry and the Fayette Plateau Chamber of Commerce, they progressed and faltered, progressed and faltered.

Finally, activists and politicians hit on the idea of a National River designation for the New River. There was precedent for such a designation in the Ozarks and on the Buffalo River, and they felt it would put the New River under the umbrella of the National Park Service Organic Act of 1916. Proponents of protection for the New River loved the idea, and in 1978, President Carter signed the bill that created the New River Gorge National River and placed it forever under the protection of the National Park Service.

The most intimidating put-in there ever was: the Upper Gauley. From the moment paddles hit the water, it was on. *Whitewater Photography.*

One of that bill's proponents was a freshman congressman from Beckley, West Virginia. Nick Rahall had been active in various civic clubs since high school and was already heavily in favor of protecting the New River Gorge when he took office. He would go on to play an instrumental role in similar designation for the Gauley River, where whitewater rafting began as a casual affair.

In 1966, the Army Corps of Engineers completed the Summersville Dam and flooded the section of the Gauley River that Sayre and Jean Rodman ran on their way downstream to rapids that would eventually attract millions of visitors. Sayre described his feelings about the dam: "You will never see that run, nor will your children. When next you feel grateful for a scheduled release from the Summersville Dam, think of the once free-flowing riverbed, down in the mud under the lake. We delighted in running it, a quarter of a century ago. The dam builders took something very special from you."

(A funny little story sheds light on the naming of the Summersville Dam, which broke the corps' long-standing tradition of naming dams and reservoirs after flooded towns. In this case, that town was Gad, West Virginia. They opted pretty quickly against the name "Gad Dam.")

Nevertheless, as far as the corps was concerned, boaters were welcome on the river. They simply didn't care what went on downstream of their dam.

And indeed, the local men who worked at the dam had a relaxed relationship with boaters, both private and commercial. Paul Breuer made friends with a dam employee named Jack Dorsey, who warmed up easily to a fresh cup of coffee. Breuer rolled up to the dam one morning and, coffee in hand, introduced himself to Dorsey and said, "Hey what's going on? We're new in town and just trying to understand all this and how it works."

The resulting relationship would prove beneficial to boating, as Breuer continued to approach Dorsey on subsequent occasions to ask for more water. "We would call up and say, 'Hey Jack, looks like it's about two thousand cfs. We'd sure like twenty-eight hundred,'" recalled Breuer.

"Yeah," Jack often responded, "I can handle that for you."

That relationship, however, was not to last.

In 1981, the Army Corps of Engineers announced its intention to build a long-tunnel hydroelectric project at the Summersville Dam. Its proposal was to pipe water from the lake three miles downhill and into a hydroelectric generator and then release it back into the Gauley River. The bottom line for boaters was that the project would have dewatered the first three miles of the Gauley.

A club of private boaters, the West Virginia Wildwater Association (WVWA), was the first to spring into action. Kim and Aggie Casto were two WVWA members who met through the organization and became key members of an activist group that soon spun off with its own nonprofit status. Together with Ed Rhett, Chris Dragan of Wildwater Unlimited, Don Weidemann, Paul Breuer of Mountain River Tours, Pope Barrow, Steve Taylor, Dave Brisell and Charlie Walbridge, they called themselves Citizens for the Gauley River (CFGR).

CFGR undertook a wide range of grassroots activism, including driving around the countryside in a pickup truck with signs and simply speaking to people to educate them about the corps' intentions. They sold T-shirts and started the Gauley Festival to raise money. One early Gauley Festival poster had a corps employee in a military uniform stylized as an evil giant with his hand on the valve, while tiny kayakers cowered in the background. An estimated two to three thousand people attended that festival, and the CFGR folk were blown away by the support. "Gauley Festival was so successful as a fundraiser," said Kim Casto, "that AWA [American Whitewater Association, now shortened to American Whitewater] took it over after we were done." That festival continues annually as Gauley Fest.

In the beginning, however, CFGR was alone in the wilderness, a tiny, quiet voice versus the United States Army. The corps did not view downstream recreation as any of its business. Instead, the corps maintained, its project purposes were low-flow augmentation and flood control.

Surprisingly, even the rafting companies didn't seem all that interested in joining the effort to fight the long-tunnel project. The corps had told them that the project would be good for their businesses, and some reluctantly agreed.

"We thought, okay, we can't just be a bunch of river runners against this project," said Aggie Casto. "It was crucial that we have the outfitters. They had a huge amount of clout."

"The corps was trying to convince them that they could make money off the project," she continued. "We had to prove to them that they weren't going to gain financially. Once we were able to do that, they were behind us."

There was more to the equation, however, than mere money.

Jim Zoia is a longtime congressional aide who served under Nick Rahall as chief of staff of the House Natural Resources Committee. "At the time," said Zoia, "the corps was blackmailing the outfitters into supporting the project."

Zoia does not use the term blackmail lightly. "It was happening! They basically were telling the outfitters—not in writing—but they were telling the outfitters that if you don't back us on this long-tunnel proposal, then we're not going to give you releases. They were releasing the water in the middle of the night!"

It was a report by Steve Taylor of CFGR, a scientist with expertise in cost-benefit ratios and hydrology, that finally changed the outfitters' minds. "The information was convincing enough to them that what the corps was telling them didn't add up," said Kim. "If he could not have

Lady Bird Johnson on the New River, 1976. *Butch Christian Collection.*

convinced them, it would have been lost." That report made it clear that the corps' estimation of impact downstream was wildly incorrect and that a regular schedule of releases from the Summersville Dam was entirely capable of fulfilling the corps' other project purposes.

With the outfitters on board, CFGR approached Jon Dragan to run the organization, but he felt that it needed somebody who could give it more time and who had more experience working against the Corps of Engineers.

That person was David Brown, who at the time headed up EPRO, the Eastern Professional River Outfitters. Fresh off a major victory against a Tennessee Valley Authority hydroelectric project on the Ocoee River in southeastern Tennessee, Brown was eager to help.

Under Brown, CFGR set about gaining the support of as many interested groups as possible and developing a strategy to overcome the corps' belligerence. Miners were convinced that hydroelectric would displace coal jobs, so they joined the effort. Despite corps promises of a new trout fishery, anglers jumped on board as well. "I think they were catching pretty big trout under current conditions," said Brown.

"The Corps of Engineers had a public meeting at Nicholas County High School," said Kim, "and the place was just packed. The majority of them were coal miners."

CFGR took on the role of primary opposition organizer. "We had to make sure," said Aggie, "that there were letters and people against it over the course of time. That's what we did."

The Fayette Plateau Chamber of Commerce, which recognized the Gauley River's potential to drive economic development, soon joined the mix as well.

However, "the thing that turned the tide," said Brown, was when Steve Taylor presented his report to Assistant Secretary of the Army (Civil Works) William Gianelli, who had oversight of the corps. "Gianelli walked in," said Brown, "and goes, 'I know all about you whiteriver rafters.'" Nevertheless, Taylor's report was indisputable, and in terms of regular releases, "the corps turned around 180 degrees as a result of that meeting."

On long-tunnel hydroelectric, however, the corps was still not moved.

CFGR and outfitters were not without support in the federal government. "We recognized back then that this was not only an outstanding recreational resource but one which could contribute to the local economy," said Zoia.

Congressman Rahall was firmly on the side of CFGR and the outfitters. "In the Energy and Water Appropriations Act, that would have been 1985, I inserted a provision to make whitewater recreation on the Gauley River a project purpose of the Summersville Dam as administered by the Corps of Engineers," he said. That bill passed and defeated the Summersville Dam long-tunnel proposal once and for all.

To Kim and Aggie Casto, when victory finally happened, it came quickly and suddenly. "I don't ever remember feeling good about it until it happened," said Aggie. "We loved the river. And we were foolish enough to believe that our voices counted. Sometimes they just need to be the right voices, so we just worked at getting the right voices saying the same thing."

The 1985 provision was historic in that it was the first time whitewater recreation became an official Corps of Engineers project purpose. Rahall and crew followed it up with the Water Resources Development Act of 1986, which made the Gauley's autumn water release schedule part of federal law. It's still the schedule now, weekends only and during the day, also known as Gauley Season.

Still, federal protection of the Gauley River was not a foregone conclusion for all time. Interested parties, including Congressman Rahall, recognized that there was still potential for other interests to threaten the Gauley. "We came to a point in 1987," said Zoia, "where Congressman Rahall said we've got to put this to bed for good. And the way to do this is to designate it as a unit of the National Park System." That philosophy gave rise to the West Virginia River Conservation Act of 1988, also known as the Gauley River Bill, to create the Gauley River National Recreation Area.

Zoia and his team began to contact landowners about the federal government buying their property for the park. "They're probably six big out-of-state corporate landowners in there," he said. "One of them I tracked down was a little old lady in Pittsburgh. She was the last heir." Most of the landowners were cooperative, and the Trust for Public Land bought up parcels and held them until the NPS could complete its purchases.

Democracy in Action! The Army Corps announces a public meeting in regard to whitewater releases on the Gauley River. *J. Young.*

"It was really amazing," said Zoia. "There wasn't a lot of opposition to it. I've dealt with park issues across the country, and here we were carving out a new unit of the National Park System *from private land*, and doing it with relatively little controversy."

By the time 1987 rolled around, and Congressman Rahall and others were moving to designate the Gauley as part of the National Park System, the corps had already changed its tune. "I watched the whole mindset of the corps change," said Zoia. "They became cheerleaders! They would put out releases saying how many people were going down the river and how much money it generated to the local economy."

Of the Gauley River Bill, "I recall that we had trouble getting Whitehouse approval," said Congressman Rahall. Ronald Reagan was in the Whitehouse, and it was generally against Republican philosophy to expand such protected areas. "But we had a lot of local Republican support," continued the congressman. "I recall specifically Knotts McConnell…who personally went to the Whitehouse, was a friend of Ronald Reagan's and pleaded that he sign this into law."

That bill established the largest system of federally protected waterways east of the Mississippi.

With President Reagan's signing of the Gauley River Bill, the victory against the long tunnel was complete. That was not, however, the only story of political wrangling centered on the New and Gauley Rivers.

There exists a subplot.

It's easy to paint a picture of diverse citizens meshing seamlessly to fight a perceived injustice. Some of the people involved, however, might take issue with the word "seamlessly." In fact, there was some friction between the outfitters and some members of CFGR, and surprisingly, that friction centered not on the Gauley River but on the New. At the same time various parties negotiated over Gauley policy, the NPS and the West Virginia Department of Natural Resources, which had control over outfitter licensing and customer quotas, worked with user groups to decide what to do about an undeveloped put-in halfway between Thurmond and Fayette Station at Cunard.

Outfitters wanted Cunard developed. "We were ready to close on all of the land at Cunard," said Dave Arnold of Class-VI. "We could have bought it all, but James Carrico, the first superintendent, asked us not to.

Our logic was this: we'll buy enough to keep ourselves, which we still own today, and if we let the park have the rest of it, they'll fix the road up. The road was unbelievably bad."

Some CFGR members, including Kim and Aggie Casto, were not happy at all. "Everybody wanted Cunard left alone but the outfitters," said Aggie. To them, it looked as though their partners on the Gauley—outfitters, the NPS and the DNR—had made a deal without CFGR input to improve Cunard and up the outfitters' quotas on the New River while keeping them low on the Gauley. The deal also cemented a system that exists nowhere else in America, whereby the state DNR maintains control of licenses rather than the NPS. This is huge for outfitters because they don't have to operate as park concessionaires, which carries a responsibility to comply with a host of federal regulations.

The Castos felt the New River was already crowded enough and didn't trust the outfitters to be happy with low numbers on the Gauley. "Our issue was, you don't know these guys very well, do you? They're capitalists. It's okay that they're capitalists; it's just that they're businessmen and they're going to want both. It's just a matter of time."

By the time the 1985 appropriations bill hit President Reagan's desk, much to the chagrin of the Castos, increased outfitter numbers on the New River and development of Cunard were in it.

Eventually, in 1999, the corps did get a hydroelectric plant at the Summersville Dam, but it did not include a long tunnel. The Upper Gauley run still begins at the foot of the dam. The project did physically change the way the corps releases water, however. One of the eighteen-foot Howell-Bunger valves, which previously shot water in a torrent from the base of the dam, was shut permanently. The water was diverted, and now it bubbles up from under the surface. Though the project had no practical effect on those plying the Gauley, it forever changed its put-in from a clamorous monster to a silent one. Rafters still leap from land directly into Class-IV water, but now, for better or worse, they can hear themselves think while doing it.

The Federal Energy Regulatory Commission approved the permit for Summersville Dam hydroelectric in 1992, and as public hearings progressed for it, the Nicholas County sheriff, a man known as Sarge, again wielded a heavy hand against the whitewater industry. Sarge owned a dive shop on Summersville Lake, and the Gauley Season autumn releases muddied his water. The last thing he wanted was for the outfitters to somehow finagle extra scheduled releases in the spring and summer.

Sarge invited Class-VI's Jeff Proctor into a dark, smoky back room at his dive shop for a talk. He made it very clear that if the outfitters made any attempt to gain scheduled flows other than what they were already getting, "we were toast," said Proctor. Sarge went on to explain that if the outfitters maneuvered for anything other than what they already had, his deputies would begin to apply the entire 181-page West Virginia vehicle inspection book to every single raft bus that turned in toward the dam.

"It'll take three or four hours per vehicle to get to the dam," Proctor reported Sarge saying to him.

Today, there are still no scheduled spring and summer releases on the Gauley River.

THE RUBBER ROOM

There exists a fellowship of raft guides that is largely unspoken and ill defined yet ever-present nonetheless. Sometimes friendships grow gradually over the course of working many trips together. Other times, respect between guides is forged in foam and hammered out upon an anvil of stone, all in a matter of minutes. One such story took place in 1998 at the Keeney Brothers rapids, where Larry Nibert and Doug Ludwig became fast friends.

When the water on the New River is high, the three Keeney rapids merge into one and become the longest and arguably most dangerous rapid on the river. Boats begin on the right side at Upper Keeney, where they float past Whale Rock on the left. If the water isn't too high, and Whale Rock isn't Whale *Hole*, there's an eddy behind it. It can be difficult to break into that eddy, but the pool of slower, calmer water can help guide a boat leftward to line up for Middle Keeney, which is choked with huge, surging, irregular waves, even on the cleanest line. The one wave most people try like mad to avoid is the Pipeline, aka the Mouth Wave. It's steep and massive, and if you catch it at the wrong moment, it is also quite mean.

If a boater swims in Middle Keeney, he doesn't have a lot of time before the current pulls him into a jumble of rocks at center right at the top of Lower Keeney called the Meat Grinder. There may not be a worse place to be on the New River at high water. Those rocks, the angriest of which is Flint Rock, form several cracks that are large enough to let water through but small enough to trap a person. It has been the site of at least one death.

The cleanest line there passes the Meat Grinder well to the left and into Lower Keeney. That doesn't mean the left is completely safe, however. At the bottom of Lower Keeney, just when you think everything will surely turn out okay, there's a massive wave called Lollygag. It's possible to run Lollygag cleanly, but out of a boat it would be a horrible, terrifying swim, after which the swimmer might very well meet his dead ancestors waiting at the end.

Most people call Larry Nibert "Redneck." Note the capital *R*. The moniker is not an insult, however. It's a nickname, and Redneck wears it as well as a West Virginia boy can. That is to say, it fits him, and it's neither good nor bad that people call him that. They just do, and he answers to it.

Nibert makes an odd pairing with Doug Ludwig. Ludwig doesn't look big until you get right up next to him, and then he's larger than life. His brown hair falls past the middle of his back, and his beard is wild enough to look longer than it actually is. He's the spitting image of the southern white Jesus.

Nibert was working for Rivers at the time, where very few people had advanced swift-water rescue skills. "We had the basics," he said. "CPR, first aid. But I was considered pretty much the senior staff." This got a hearty laugh from Ludwig.

"I was leading a five- or six-boat trip that day," continued Nibert, as he ignored Doug. "My next experienced boater was a two-year guide. So, I had a bunch of first- and second-year boaters. The river was probably seven and a half feet."

"Eight and a half is what I remember," said Ludwig.

"It was big water," agreed Nibert.

"In my boat, I had a group of three and some family members, who worked at a restaurant," he continued. "And needless to say, they quit growing up a long time ago. They'd been growing *out* for a while. I took a load of nine people, which happened a lot in those days."

Nibert was running first, which is common among trip leaders at many raft companies.

Several times over the years, other more experienced boaters had attempted to teach him the standard raft line at Upper Keeney, but "all

A borrowed army-surplus bridge raft carrying twelve men and *maybe* three paddles barely survives a run-in with Flint Rock in the Meat Grinder, Lower Keeney rapid on the New River, 1972. No beer was harmed in the making of this photograph. *Butch Christian Collection.*

I'd ever done was just go left," said Nibert. His approach to it had always been successful before, and indeed, "just go left" is pretty much exactly what the standard line is. That time, however, the angle of his boat was a hair off, and such things are not typically trivial in big, pushy water. Nibert moved to put the nose of his boat into the eddy behind Whale Rock to slow things down and move him left for Middle Keeney, but the eddy had other plans. "I go to break into the eddy behind Whale Rock, and it knocks me out. I keep trying to break into the eddy, and each time, it knocks me out. I'm like, 'I'm not going to make this move.'"

"So I thought, 'Okay, what do I do?'"

Nibert yelled to his crew, "Alright guys, hard forward! Hard forward! Get ready for a get down! Get ready for a get down!" Nibert squared his boat up on the towering Mouth Wave, and just as he plowed into it, he shouted "GET DOWN!"

"And I ain't kidding you," said Nibert, "that boat stood up as vertical as it could. It kicked around in the air like a musky trying to kick a plug, and everybody left the boat but me. *God* kept me in that boat. There must have been stick 'um on my butt."

About that time, Ludwig's trip came into view, and he saw what had happened downstream. "It looked like he was flipping," said Ludwig. "It did a big kick up. It kicked to the left, and everybody went shooting that way."

"There's probably only been about three times or four times that I've ever hit something, where I felt like it was running into a brick wall," pointed out Nibert for effect. "That thing couldn't have broke on me more perfect."

"So, I'm screaming every expletive known to man to get my point across to people swimming right, people swimming left, and believe it or not, I picked up somewhere around six or seven people myself," beamed Nibert. He couldn't get them all, however, and there was nobody downstream to assist him. He and his crew were on their own.

The boat and its spilled cargo rapidly approached the Meat Grinder, but Nibert was hardly green himself, and he thought quickly. "I make a move around *to the right* of Flint Rock into an eddy and go down backward," he said. "My head's going a hundred different directions. I look around, and somebody swam through Lollygag. Another raft picks them up."

Nibert's flotilla spent the next quarter mile picking up people and equipment and finally pulled over for a breather just before the next big rapid, Dudley's Dip. "And that's when I realize," said Nibert, "I'm missing someone."

"I had a boatload of weak paddlers, too," said Ludwig, "with one strong guy. He's riding front left for me, and I'm rowing. I've got all greenie raft guides behind me."

Ludwig saw Nibert's boat spit out its crew, but he wasn't initially close enough to help. However, "we come through past there, and I look right and see somebody *hanging onto Meat Grinder*. This dude is hugging it."

One of the Meat Grinder rocks has a small lip on the top of it, which, at eight and a half feet, is just under water. The man had somehow managed to grab the lip as the current raked him over it. After a few tense moments, he hoisted himself up, climbed atop the rock and stood there with the water at his ankles, surging to his knees. Since it was just under the water, the rock was not, technically speaking, even an island. Class-V river raged all around him for many meters in every direction. He was desperately stuck, a sopping and forlorn near-victim of the New River.

Ludwig caught the same eddy that had just pushed Nibert's boat to the right of the Meat Grinder, but he had never been there before and didn't know what to expect. It is common wisdom that if you're in this particular eddy, you *are* going to the right of Meat Grinder, whether you want to or not. But then, rules are meant to be broken.

Ludwig examined the situation. He looked back upstream to see where his other guides were and if they could offer any assistance. No luck. All three of the other boats had committed to Lower Keeney and were either on their way into it or already there. Ludwig spared a moment to see if they would be okay…just in time to watch one of them flip in Lollygag. "I'm in a bind, you know? I don't want to commit to Meat Grinder to get this guy, but I know my trip is getting trashed."

He decided on the only course of action that didn't involve abandoning Nibert's crewman to the Meat Grinder. Ludwig cupped his hands to his mouth and yelled, "Hey, I'm gonna come get you! When I come by, jump in the boat!" He turned his boat diagonally upstream, got his oars moving at a furious pace and ferried out sideways in front of the carnage, intending to stay just upstream of it while fighting fast water all the way.

"I passed that boat so close, he could have just stepped onto it. I took it right past that lip. *And he didn't move.* And I was like, well, this is it, dude."

At the last moment, his already risky plan falling apart at the seams, Ludwig caught the man's eye and screamed, "JUMP! JUMP!"

The man leapt for the boat, caught the raft's outer tube in the chest and barely hung on. One of Ludwig's guests leapt into action and grabbed the soaked man, pulling him the rest of the way into the boat in the nick of time.

His boat, however, was not out of trouble. The Meat Grinder is a third of the river wide, and it was obvious to Ludwig that he was not going to make it safely around. "At this point," said Ludwig, "I'm thinking, 'Oh, this is bad—sideways in an oar rig.'" He cranked his oars franticly—back on the left and forward on the right—to turn the boat just enough to get a forty-five-degree angle. Miraculously, they made it past the pour-overs without losing anybody. Inches made the difference.

After all that, "my next thought is, where is everybody?" said Ludwig. "I look down the river, and it's like a ghost town. There's *nobody*. No helmets, no paddles floating, nothing. I had a three-boat trip; Redneck had four or five boats. Nothing. Finally, we come around the bend."

Nibert spent several minutes coming to grips with the fact that one of his guests was missing in the river. For a raft guide, the only thing worse would be two missing people. His stomach was in his throat. He thought he had killed somebody.

"Then, here comes Jesus around the corner, with these oars," laughed Nibert, remembering both what he saw and his relief at seeing it.

Ludwig yelled out, "Hey, you missing something?"

"And just about that time," said Nibert, "Jesus realizes I've got something that belongs to him."

"He's got my whole freaking trip," said Ludwig. "I cleaned up his stuff. He cleaned up mine. And ever since then, we've been cool."

Dragan developed a method for his huge New River rafts that involved a guide at the stern and one at the bow. Here, Butch Christian draw strokes from the stern, while Hillary Jones pries from the bow on Pillow Rock rapid, Gauley River. *Butch Christian Collection.*

In this photo, the raft falls neatly into the Toilet Bowl at Pillow Rock rapid, which is actually a good thing. *Butch Christian Collection.*

It may very well be that raft guides are the lowest-paid professional athletes anywhere, but the promise of Doug-and-Larry-style adventure—sometimes delivered, sometimes not—drives no small number of people to give up all semblance of a normal life and settle into one of backbreaking work for little or no money. It's like seeing the cartoon version of an insane person wearing a ball gag and chains and thinking, "I want that!" They even get a rubber room of sorts—a raft—in which to spend their days.

Even at the dawn of the industry, many raft guides were born and bred West Virginians who grew up around the river but never ran it—that would be plum crazy—and didn't know the first thing about guiding a raft when they started out. They just saw a bizarre new thing that people were traveling from all over to do on a river, and that their parents told them could kill them, and they wanted more than anything to be part of it.

In 1979, one of them was eighteen-year-old Michael Ivey. "It had started to impact our psyches even in high school," said Ivey. "We pretty

The raft industry boomed at least in part because the West Virginia Department of Commerce brought in journalists by the truckload to write about it. Here, Butch Christian (front row, second from right) poses with a team from *National Geographic*, 1975. *Butch Christian Collection.*

much knew it was the place to be, because these people always had a party going on, and there were always women showing up from out of state who had valid plastic."

Ivey started out with a friend, Danny Ballard, whose brother, Randall, owned a small raft company called Drift-a-Bit. They did not, however, begin their whitewater careers on the river. Ivey and Ballard worked out of an abandoned bank building in Glen Jean, printing T-shirts to sell to outfitters. "We were hustling around, trying to make some money, both artistic kinda guys," said Ivey. He is one of four children in his family. Two of his siblings joined the military. "It wasn't like there was opportunity in this part of Appalachia," he said. "It was sort of like this permanent recession. I saw it as an opportunity to make some money and get a job. I'm sure we would have been coal miners had we the opportunity to make that 60k a year at the time. We tried to do something with art, which wasn't the worst decision, but we really weren't businesspeople."

Their biggest-selling T-shirt said: "Wet Your Pants in the New River."

Ivey first ran whitewater in 1980 with New River Scenic Whitewater Tours, a company based in Hinton, West Virginia. It was something he might never have done were it not for various forces of nature, namely being nineteen and wanting to hook up. He had never been on the water before. "I was pretty terrified of it," he said. "Luckily, you wore a life jacket, and nobody ever asked me if I could swim. It was a motivating factor: to party with the tourists."

Soon enough, he was guiding for his former partner's brother.

Ivey became addicted to the freedom inherent in the job, and he was not alone. "That freedom of being your own boss," he mused, "'cause once you're in that boat alone, you're your own boss—I think that's kind of what these West Virginia people liked." Plus, with Ballard, he was in a fledgling company, which was just plain fun. "We would actually have 'work parties,'" he said, "which I think now is hilarious. You got paid in beer and hot dogs, and you built stuff. You built the equipment the business used."

Some guides loved the river life but either grew tired of guiding or just never saw the allure. Many became video boaters, a role that got them paid to paddle but didn't require them to be people persons. A whole segment of the industry grew up around providing videos and photos of guests in major rapids, with faces either aglow from the rush of adrenaline or awash with spume.

Ivey soon learned a lesson that the vast majority of people who join the rafting industry to make money learn: they would never get rich doing it. He had no idea when he started out that in his best year, he would barely crack $10,000, half of which were tips.

It's always difficult to generalize, but if there are three traits that seem to characterize many river guides, they are the desire to make money; a willingness not to, as long there's plenty of fun to be had; and the drive to party. That third trait has been constant throughout the history of the industry. There are only two types of motor vehicles in which it is still legal in West Virginia to carry open alcohol containers: limousines and raft buses.

One company, Rivers, built its business around that drive. When Rivers decided it wanted to be a full-service resort, its owner, Fast Eddie Lilly, asked himself, what does a resort need?

The answers were obvious. A resort needs a restaurant, a place to sleep and a place to drink. Lilly built rustic camping cabins, which were essentially wooden tents. Those cabins were Spartan to say the least. Guests had a modicum of privacy, bunks and perhaps a light bulb, but they were "cabins in the woods," and who doesn't want to spend the weekend in a cabin in the woods? Where Rivers really excelled was in the drinking, specifically in a bar, called the Red Dog Saloon, at its campus a quarter of the way into the New River Gorge.

"It was packed full of energy," Ivey remembered fondly. "There were people dancing on the tables. It was wild, man, just fun. And once in a while it was rough, too, because local people started invading, and they didn't understand the river. They just came for the drinking. It became sort of this hybrid river bar meets local bar that got really crazy."

Somehow—nobody is really sure how—Lilly drew some pretty big-name rock 'n' roll acts to his campus in the gorge. Blue Oyster Cult and Steppenwolf both played there, and neither was far past the height of its popularity.

"The social phenomenon of the Red Dog occurred because Rivers had a clientele that was showing up to get ripped," said Ivey. "It was the one amenity you could offer that was pretty easy."

Despite the glamour of guiding and the fact that there was a party pretty much every night in season, the ego trip that was driving a raft paled under the harsh glare of extreme poverty and body-breaking hard work. "It became a job," he said. "I have friends now who are former professional athletes, and I wonder—what did that guy do at the same time I was running the river? Well, he probably made a couple hundred grand a year on his worst year, when I might have made ten grand on my best year, and I had peoples' lives in my hands every day. Don't get me wrong, that's part of the draw of it, but where's the social value?"

As Ivey began to burn out on the guiding experience, he turned to other, related ventures, one of which was "Likes Your Ride, Tips Your Guide," a seminar of sorts that he led during training time at various raft companies.

There wasn't a lot of money in a raft guide's paycheck, but tips were a different story entirely. And yet it was strange, thought Ivey, how inconsistent tips were for most guides. Some raked it in. Others seemed not to do so well. Likes Your Ride attempted to analyze that incongruity, "and I realized," said Ivey, "there was a way to up your percentage of tips and your income."

Ivey broke down tip potential into a simple equation: safety plus comfort plus value equals enjoyment. He knew that safety came from training and experience.

Then came comfort. "I would always teach other guides to carry a little bigger dry bag and take some of your old warm clothes," said Ivey. "Start going to thrift stores and buy cheap wool sweaters. Even if it's little plastic ponchos that cost three bucks. And you carry little snacks, so you can boost them up. There's nothing like a little bump of sugar or some peanuts or almonds or something."

"You're the bronzed river guide," he continued,

> *because you're out there every day, but you've got white people coming out of offices. How hard is it to spend ten bucks and buy a bottle of sun screen? Carry a little kit for customers. Make sure they're warm. Make sure they have something to eat. I know some of these crews are partying hard and they're hungover. So how great is it to reach down into a bag and pull out a couple bottles of Gatorade? Talk about the love!*

Value, Ivey reasoned, comes in knowing and being able to relate certain facts about the river, like history and botany, which was a revitalization of Jon Dragan's similar philosophy. The ability to schmooze is a large part of it, too. Ivey realized that successful raft guides were social butterflies who told jokes, conversed with and got to know their guests. "It's a lot more fun to go into battle with your friends than a bunch of strangers," he said. "That kind of warmth is the hardest thing to teach. You can teach people to stock a dry bag, but can you get them to really care about those people? Those are the best river guides."

Congressman Nick Rahall agrees with the importance of a guide who is not just safe but also brings the value. "I can recall Hound Dog—and Sleepy was another one—and of course all the Proctors and Dave Arnold. I've been down with them all. Ymir, I think is retired now, Frank Lukacs...They can really tell some tales and tell some history at the same time."

Ivey also espoused the value to a guide of an educated and involved crew. Some guides made it a point of pride to take the fewest amount of paddle strokes per rapid or of moving the boat themselves, say with an oar rig. While that's what some guests want, Ivey felt it was an inferior experience for the others. Guides all learn that there is a perfect line through every rapid. If the guide puts the boat on it, the river does all the hard work, and the guests are largely unnecessary to the run. "You can turn your own raft and set your own angles and keep your boat on that line," said Ivey, "but it's not nearly as much fun as hitting that wave as hard as eight people digging in can possibly hit it."

"This is one difference between western and eastern guides," he continued.

> *If you want to run like a western guide and act like you've got a center-mount oar rig on a pig boat and those people are just dead weight, then that's what you do. It's probably safe and it's still going down the river, but that's not eastern guiding. That's not the way I came up with. You've got eight motors sitting in front of you, and there are so many places where it's all about that raft going vertical.*

Ivey soon picked up other skills, in addition to training. He taught himself photography and design and was soon creating brochures for raft companies. Rivers' brochure became the first of those when Ivey bumped into Eddie Lilly on a gambling junket to Atlantic City. "Hey, man, I might need some pictures," said Lilly simply.

Eventually, Ivey parlayed his experiences into a real career as a designer, photographer and filmmaker, which he still enjoys today, and that's been a common pattern among West Virginia raft guides since the beginning. Many still live in the area and make their livings using skills, such as video production, marketing or management, that they never would have learned were it not for their lives in the rubber room.

THE SCORE

As rafters on the Lower New River wend their way northward, they eventually happen upon a long, calm pool. Sunshine floods the valley with warmth there, and people leap from their boats to grab a swim and drift in the lazy current. At the downstream end of the pool, visible from over a mile away, the New River Gorge Bridge towers above all, especially its tiny cousin underneath it, the Fayette Station Bridge.

Tourists switchback their way down the steep north side of the gorge and cross the Fayette Station Bridge on their way to a parking area and gravel beach on river left. Fayette Station draws crowds of onlookers in the summertime because, one, it's easily accessible by vehicle and, two, it sits just ashore of Fayette Station rapid, a cranking Class-III/IV train of haystack waves that deliver roller-coaster thrills for boaters and gawkers alike, even well into the low-water season.

There are actually two beaches at Fayette Station. The first, a small sandy patch, is at the very end of the long pool, just upstream of the rapid. The second, a long swath of river-polished gravel, lies just downstream of the drop and serves as the primary takeout for private boaters and many of the commercial raft companies. To gain the lower beach and pick up their tired but exhilarated guests, raft buses and trailers pass by the upper beach, cross a small bridge over Wolf Creek and drive through the tourist parking area.

At the start of 1972, however, the bridge over Wolf Creek did not exist, and the only viable takeout was the upper beach. Every boat on the river had a choice: take out just above Fayette Station and forego that last rapid or go for it.

Unfortunately, the latter necessitated an extension of the day that included far more than just one rapid. The next place to get off the river was Hawk's Nest State Park—past Hawk's Nest Lake—which meant four more miles of grueling flat water.

Where others might have seen an obstacle, Wildwater and the Dragans saw an opportunity. By purchasing the upper sandy beach, they could add the lower land into the mix, develop it and then have a takeout that would allow them to run Fayette Station. It would add a whole other rapid—a big one—to their standard Lower New River Trip. So, purchase it they did.

The first obstacle to developing the land for a takeout was Wolf Creek, and the Dragans set to work building the bridge that still spans it today. They then went to work on the land on the far side. It was choked with boulders, so they brought in crews and heavy

To enable trips in high water, Wildwater began using motorized "pig rigs." Here, a pig rig plows through standing waves on the New River. The level is somewhere around fourteen feet, or forty thousand cubic feet per second. *Butch Christian Collection.*

machinery and either crushed the rocks or moved them. Spending long, backbreaking days in the sun, they smoothed out a roadway and paved it with gravel.

When all was said and done, Wildwater spent a small fortune to purchase Fayette Station and develop it as a viable takeout. Soon, other companies began to run the Lower New, and when they did, Jon Dragan saw how easily he could begin to recoup some of the money his company had spent. He began to charge a per-person fee for other companies to take out at his beach.

Not every company bought in, however. In the beginning, Mountain River Tours and Appalachian Wildwaters refused to pay Dragan's fees and instead braved the long paddle out to Hawk's Nest. Class-VI started out that way, too, for the first three years of its operation.

"From day one it was, when you ran the New River, Jon Dragan put on his big boots and said I own the [expletive deleted] river," said Imre Szilagyi of AW. "He claimed to own all the put-ins and takeouts, so we found ways around him…He pretty well had Fayette Station locked up."

There were dozens of commercial outfitters rafting the New River then. Some ate Dragan's fees. Some devised creative, but ultimately inefficient and sometimes unsuccessful, ways to take out near Fayette Station.

Rivermen, for one, incorporated in 1980 without a way to get off the river. The company's founder, Steve Campbell, wanted to sign a lease at Dragan's property, but according to Jon, they were full. He would allow no more companies to take out there. Campbell called the West Virginia Department of Transportation, which maintained the road and bridge at the bottom of the gorge just upstream of Fayette Station rapid, for advice. He asked them if he could legally use the state's right of way under the road to beach his boats and walk up public property to a waiting vehicle. The state saw no issues with the plan, so Campbell and his company began to exit the river on the tiny sliver of public land that defines the boundaries of the road.

Other companies soon followed suit. Some of them even devised complicated pulley systems to haul their heavy boats up to the bridge.

Rivermen continued to take out under the bridge for its first year of operation before finally signing a lease with another property owner just upstream on river right. As he made his way to his new takeout early that year, Campbell pulled in to find No Trespassing signs nailed to trees—facing the river. "I just assumed Jon didn't think we had a lease on any of it," he said. "I took the signs down and posted them on his takeout facing the river, so when *his* customers came in the next time, they saw those same signs," laughed Campbell.

In 1984, Rivermen finally signed a Dragan lease, but its four seasons prior to that were typical of how small companies had to operate—without a way to get off the water legally, they simply couldn't run trips.

Szilagyi made a deal to have a motorized boat meet his trips at the top of Hawk's Nest Lake and tow his rafts to the takeout. When the arrangement worked, it worked well, but as West Virginia machinery is wont to do, the outboards didn't always run, and sometimes the tow boat never showed. It was a less than optimal situation, but AW guides grinned and bore it. "When the river was minus four feet, and you got down to the lake and the tow boat wasn't there," recalled Szilagyi, "that's a long, long way."

Even the most acidic well will eventually run dry, and Hawk's Nest Lake was no different. When MRT incorporated in 1973, Paul Breuer also chose to paddle or tow to Hawk's Nest. Once there, his teams would load their rafts onto the tourist tram that leads up to the rim of the gorge, board buses and head for the hills. That arrangement was the first to fail. "They got pretty upset about it," said Breuer, "because it was getting the tram and the other people riding it all wet." Hawk's Nest told MRT they couldn't use the tram anymore, so instead, they began to drive their buses all the way down to the river for the pickup. That was also a less than optimal situation. "It was a pretty scary drive. It's a one-lane gravel road on the side of a cliff! You can't pass but three or four places within a mile."

Finally, in 1980, the Hawk's Nest State Park pulled the plug on the entire enterprise and told MRT that it would no longer be allowed to drive its buses on the road. "Where do you take out?" shrugged Breuer. "Jon Dragan."

Eight years after the purchase of Fayette Station, most companies paid Jon Dragan. Wildwater was firmly in control of access to and egress from the river, and that may have been the plan all along. "We did it because Jon had the foresight to buy property," said Tom Dragan.

That land purchase would prove to be the first of many by West Virginia rafting companies and a major factor in whether or not they would be successful down the road. The effects of Wildwater's Fayette Station deal still ripple throughout the industry today. It quite literally changed the business model of most existing outfitters and many of those to follow.

The first companies to learn the real estate lesson were those that were running to Hawk's Nest or paying Wildwater's fees.

Even as egress at Hawk's Nest turned less and less certain, the fee structure at Fayette Station also began to seem unsustainable. Companies that were paying for egress balked at what they perceived to be exorbitant fees and draconian rules for use of the land. "We spent '78, '79 and '80 taking out at Hawk's Nest," said Doug Proctor of Class-VI. "Then we signed an agreement with Wildwater to take out at Fayette Station. We did that for three years, and the price was a buck fifty per person, two fifty, then three dollars—with an escalator."

"The price structure was all written down in the agreement at the very beginning," Tom Dragan pointed out. "It started off at a dollar a head, so they could get used to it, because they were taking out at Hawk's Nest for nothing."

"Plus there were all sorts of restrictions," noted Breuer. "If your bus goes over fifteen miles per hour, you're out of here. On and on and on."

"And on top of paying that amount," added Proctor, "there was pressure to vote certain ways on various river access issues. Really, Wildwater was in control of the whole industry. So, we decided to look for an alternative, and that was going to be the Teay's project."

After several years of paying rising fees to take out at Fayette Station, four outfitters said enough is enough. In early 1981, Breuer suggested building a takeout on the other side of the river and about a mile downstream at an old mining site called Teay's Landing. "We were convinced," said Breuer, "Frank Lukacs [North American River Runners], Imre [Appalachian Wildwaters] and I…Dave Arnold [Class-VI] and Jeff…that we needed to do this. We needed to own our own fate because Jon was making thousands and thousands and holding us hostage."

The way the Fayette Station deal with Wildwater was structured, on February 1 of every year, the lease for takeouts renewed automatically. On January 31, unless a lessee had hand-delivered a letter saying his company was out of the deal, they were in for another year. AW, NARR and MRT all sent their letters. Catfish Whelan drove down to deliver Class-VI's. Jon Dragan was there, and by the look on his face and the tone of his voice, it was obvious to Whelan that he already knew the outfitters were jumping ship. "That was the point of no return," said Proctor. "We had to be successful."

There was an obstacle, however, between the old Ames mine site and the river: the CSX rail line. Even as the outfitters burned their bridges with Wildwater, they still didn't have permission from the railroad company to cross its land. And getting that permission was far from a sure thing. The line was one of CSX's busiest, and shutting it down for several days equated to a multimillion-dollar loss. And yet, the 1981 commercial raft season was mere months away. "We had cut off the limb," said Breuer, "and we were falling to ground."

"The only way to get to the river was to put a tunnel under the railroad," said Dave Arnold of Class-VI, "because the railroad was not going to let you cross it. One or two people walking across? They can close their eyes. But you have 100,000 people carrying rafts, and they're obviously going to say cease and desist eventually."

Together, the outfitters knew enough people with landholdings at Teay's to approach about a purchase. Breuer began work on the engineering of the tunnel along with a materials supplier, Armco Steel. Frank Lukacs had political ties to CSX because, apparently, one NARR guide's father was high up in the company.

By February 1, the team had already figured out much of the logistics of building the tunnel. The steel was lined up and ready to go, and the coalition easily obtained a $500,000 loan to pay for it all. "The irony of the whole thing is that it was bankable," said Arnold. "Jon was charging us so much money, that we could go to the bank and finance a half-million-dollar deal because, look, we're already paying it."

As February turned to March, the coalition had financing. They had the engineering and materials lined up. "We had everything in place except for one thing," said Arnold, "permission from the railroad to go under."

It was obviously in Wildwater's interest to stop the coalition from building the tunnel, so Dragan hired a lobbyist to work on his company's behalf.

"Jon tried to put extraordinary pressure on us," said Arnold. He invited Arnold and Proctor down to Thurmond to talk—without the other coalition members. "Basically, he tried to leverage us to break the coalition." Dragan told Arnold and Proctor that he would let Class-VI back in, even though they missed the February 1 cutoff. All they had to do was walk away from the other three outfitters. "It scared the hell out of Doug and I. I remember driving out, coming up Dun Loop; Doug and I were almost shaking."

"We knew if we jumped ship, our fathers would kill us!" said Proctor.

The coalition in turn hired Arch Moore, a former and future West Virginia governor, to handle its legal work. The outfitters knew they needed a big gun, somebody who could call up CSX and get a face-to-face meeting with its president, John Snow (who would eventually become U.S. secretary of the treasury under George W. Bush). No mere river hippie could get an audience with Snow, so Moore's main role was to negotiate with CSX. There were rumors that he was set to run for governor again, which couldn't hurt matters.

The coalition knew that it was Snow, and nobody else, who had to make the call to shut down the track. Nobody below him would dare to make the decision, because if somebody said yes, his or her job would have been forfeit.

The clock ticked on, and the season loomed like an execution date, but the outfitters were committed. "We actually ordered the steel and had it delivered to the site," said Arnold. "And the railroad freaked out. They said, 'What are you doing!?' We said, 'You don't understand, we have no choice. We've cut our ties.'"

"Our gamble was this: Would the state really let us go bankrupt? Would they really let four companies in a growth industry go down?"

Actually, there was little doubt that CSX would allow the work to happen. The question was *how* would they allow it to proceed? Would they allow an open cut, for which the track would have to be shut down, so the coalition could complete the job in one frenzied push? That's certainly what the coalition wanted because it meant they could put the job behind them sooner and start running trips. Or was CSX going to tell them that they could only shut the track down for a few hours a day? The latter would have prolonged the project over the course of the summer, preventing any of the companies from running trips and likely spelling the demise of all four.

"We needed an open seventy-two-hour window," said Proctor simply. But as opening weekend of raft season drew nigh—and tunnel construction weekend even more so—the team still didn't have a yes from CSX.

Dave Arnold said, "I was in a meeting at the state DNR, and I knew that was the day Arch was going to have a heart-to-heart with Mr. Snow. In the meeting, I get handed a note from the secretary. It said, 'The tunnel has been denied.'"

"That's all it said. I'm sure I turned white and probably looked like I was about to vomit. It meant we were going down. The director of the DNR looked at me and said, 'Dave, are you okay? Do we need to take a break?'"

Arnold called his partner, Jeff Proctor, and asked what was going on. "It doesn't look good," replied Proctor.

The conversation between Arch Moore and John Snow had been brief. During the meeting, Snow expressed his denial of permission to build the tunnel, to which Moore reportedly replied, "That's fine, as long as you understand the score is CSX one, me nothing. Thanks for your time." And he left.

Crestfallen and morose, Arnold went back into the meeting. Not that any of it mattered. With no permission to build the tunnel, his company was sunk anyway. However, "it wasn't five minutes more," he said, "the secretary comes up with another note, and it says, 'The tunnel has been approved.' I said, 'I need to take another break.'"

Minutes after the meeting between Moore and Snow had concluded, and Moore had stalked out of the office angry, Snow called him back and reportedly said, "You know Arch, I've been thinking about it. We really don't like that score. We're going to give you the open trench. You've got seventy-two hours on Memorial Day Weekend."

"So, we had seventy-two hours," said Proctor. They pulled it off in fifty-six hours, working three shifts a day.

In their biggest years, fees paid to Wildwater for taking out at Fayette Station would have been in the neighborhood of $60,000 to $80,000 a year. "Hindsight says, it was probably stupid," said Tom Dragan. "Hindsight says we should have charged two bucks a head and let them

Tom Dragan, brother of the late Jon Dragan, stands next to the Thurmond Union Church, which served as the Wildwater offices for several years. *J. Young.*

run as many people on the river as they wanted. We'd have made four times as much money and never had to run a raft trip."

Right or wrong, fair or unfair, however, Dragan's fees were less about greed and more about encouraging what he felt was healthy pricing for the industry as a whole. By tying his fees to other companies' rates, he could keep a handle on their prices, which he felt should remain low. "He used to say, 'If everybody charged the same amount, then you wouldn't have a problem,'" said Melanie Dragan.

At the time, there was also talk of upping the maximum number of people allowed to run the river per day, but Jon Dragan didn't want those numbers to increase. He could block it simply by limiting the number of people he would let take out at Fayette Station. Even if the Dragans had kept Fayette Station fees low, Tom believes the coalition would still have built the Teay's tunnel because his brother would never have yielded on that number.

"When they got the other side, their price structure [for other companies to take out] was identical to ours," Tom pointed out. "They did the same thing we did, and nobody went over there because the prices were the same. Were *our* prices too high? For them they were. But when the shoe was on the other foot, it wasn't as big a deal. And we did maintain that [maximum] number on the river until the Park Service bought us."

Jon Dragan eventually sold Wildwater's land at Fayette Station and the put-in at Stone Cliff above Thurmond to the National Park Service, and in so doing, he got the last word. Dragan made sure to include provisions in the sale to ensure that everybody who put in at Stone Cliff and took out at Fayette Station—including commercial outfitters—would always be able to do so, and now they pay nothing. "Here this conglomerate went and spent a million dollars on a tunnel," laughed Melanie sweetly, "and now all these people could take out across the river for nothing."

The lesson the industry learned as a whole, however, was more valuable than a hundred tunnels. "A light bulb went off," said Proctor. "Long-term leases and especially owning property on and around the river was critical. It's a real estate game." They applied the lesson liberally on the New River and, just as importantly, on the Gauley.

MRT, for one, already owned land there. Early on, MRT was running trips on the Gauley on a regular basis, and when a plot of land, river left at Wood's Ferry, came up for tax sale, it borrowed $1,000 from a local attorney to add to its own funds and snatched it up.

That property needed work over the course of years to be viable, however. The road was only graveled for a mile off the hard top of Saturday Road, and the rest of it was in terrible shape. "The road had slid in, and there was a log on one side that we had to walk over originally to get to the river," said Breuer. "We used wheelbarrows to get our rafts down there."

One Class-VI acquisition was a permanent right of way to access a natural gas pipeline at Panther Mountain, down which they slid their rafts to the river for a number of years. "In 1979, we were looking for a way to get on the Lower Gauley," said Proctor, "and all of a sudden we go out there and there's this pipe. We used to blow our rafts up at the top, and we're talking six hundred feet…we just set the rafts on the pipe and walked on down."

"It worked remarkably well," added Arnold. "To this day, if you cleared all the briars, you could do it, piece of cake." Class-VI still owns a legal right to cross that property and access the pipe. "The gas company was really kind of glad because they had to go up and down that thing all the time. And we built the road—they could drive to the halfway point."

They also still own a right of way to leap from Jump Rock. Think about that for a moment. A legal document filed in some rural courthouse somewhere actually says that Class-VI has a legal right to jump off a rock into the river.

Throughout the 1980s, Class-VI talked on and off about a land purchase with an owner called Mower Lumber. Mower owned a long tract that Class-VI wanted to buy, on river right of the Gauley from Meadow Creek at Sweet's Falls to Bucklick Branch above Koontz Bend, but to no avail. In 1987, desperate to make payroll for an upcoming month, Mower contacted Dave Arnold out of the blue and offered the tract for sale.

The purchase, which they completed in partnership with Imre Szilagyi and Appalachian Wildwaters, allowed the two companies to build river access at Mason's Branch and accomplish something they had dreamed about for years prior: splitting the formerly bisected Gauley River into thirds.

Before that purchase, there was the Upper Gauley and the Lower Gauley, and the takeout for the Upper was at Peter's Creek. "That was a long first day," said Arnold. Trisecting the river allowed them to run the "Middle" Gauley at low water in the summer, and also allowed them to adapt to high water. When heavy rains and snowmelt made the Upper Gauley too high for commercial trips, they could instead put in at Mason's Branch.

Breuer and MRT had taught the Class-VI owners the value of the Lower Gauley at high water as well, which many boaters still believe is the best whitewater run in a region filled with world-class rivers. "We were driven as guides, not as businessmen, to figure out how to run the Lower Gauley at eight grand," said Arnold.

Class-VI and AW went on to provide access at Bucklick, Mason's Branch and Wood's Ferry at river right to private boaters for twenty years. Mason's Branch and Wood's are now public property in the hands of the Park Service.

"Once we built Mason's Branch," said Arnold, "There was no way they were going back to Peter's Creek."

The same can be—and often is—said of the Cunard access point on the New River. Once that was developed, there was no way boaters would willfully put in at Thurmond at eight hundred cfs to run the Lower Gorge to Fayette Station.

Development of Cunard for public access almost certainly changed the game in terms of the growth of the industry as well, because "God knows how many guests we took down the river," said Arnold, "on a hot August day from Thurmond at one thousand cfs who got off the river and said, 'That was kinda cool, but I'm never doing it again.'"

River guides are likewise happy to have Cunard open. "If you walked out there," said Arnold, as he nodded toward the Class-VI guest sign-in area, "and said, 'Hey everybody, we're going to Thurmond for the rest of the year; we're not going to Cunard.' Talk about revolution."

"Jon Dragan made us realize that this wasn't just an outfitting game," said Proctor. "It was a real estate game." After the Teay's project, "we immediately made a decision that we were going to own every piece of land we set foot on…meaning put-ins at Meadow Creek, put-ins at Thurmond, put-ins at Prince, put-ins on the Gauley. We wanted a legal right—including lunch spots, if possible—to access the river."

THE RISE OF THE RESORTS

In 1995, the West Virginia rafting industry as a whole carried 225,446 people down the New and Gauley Rivers. It was the highest number of rafting customers ever—and remains so to this day. In fact, in 2009, that number was 139,731, a 38 percent drop in business. The industry watched helplessly as huge chunks sloughed off. Not every year since 1995 yielded a decline, but most did. It was obvious to everybody, regardless of what company they owned or worked for, that the West Virginia rafting industry—not even thirty years old—was dying.

Where were all the missing customers? The answer was painfully simple. People didn't want short-term trips anymore. Instead, vacationers were shopping for the coveted week and two-week holiday, and in droves, they began to opt for amusement parks, cruise ships and the beach over whitewater rafting.

The first companies to take the hit were smaller outfitters, which didn't have the wherewithal to stand against the ebbing tide, but even the larger outfitters knew their time in operation would be short if they didn't do something to change their business models.

Michael Ivey, who created Rivers' first real brochure, remembers Eddie Lilly of Rivers talking about the resort concept as early as when he first purchased the company. "I watched a niche of college business happen," said Ivey. "That was Eddie Lilly and Rivers. Eddie bought a company from, I think, [North American River Runners owner] Frank Lukacs's brother,

Glen. He owned the Rivers license and the property down Fayette Station Road. Eddie will credit him with having the idea of a destination resort."

At the time, Rivers enjoyed a modest weekend business model. Like all the other companies, the bulk of his customers drove into town Friday night, ran the river and partied on Saturday and then left for home on Sunday. There was very little weekday business at any of the companies, and unless a Rivers customer slept in the back of his car, his only choices for lodging were the Holiday Inn or Comfort Inn.

Jon Dragan had established a model of feeding his customers down in Thurmond at their base camp, and the other companies soon learned from his success. Raft companies began to offer a keg of beer after their trips and sometimes cooked hamburgers. "It was a really big deal," said Ivey, "when they started feeding people."

Eventually, Lilly expressed his vision of a resort to Ivey. "He wanted 'Rivers Resort complex,'" said Ivey. "He was the first guy to call it a 'resort.'"

Other companies soon wised to the notion of keeping people longer than just a weekend, but while most went for families, Rivers dove 180

Fayette Station rapid, New River, 1983: Butch Christian feels his raft get noticeably heavier as the "bucket boat" does what bucket boats did best—hold water. *Butch Christian Collection.*

degrees in the opposite direction. It wanted to be the party capital. It made its rafting a little cheaper than its competitors, threw college specials together and started wooing its customers earlier in life. "It was forty dollars," said Ivey. "You would run the river, get all the spaghetti you could eat, a few beer tokens and a place to camp for the night."

Other, non-raft-centric companies also opened or moved to the area to take advantage of the tourism trade. Terry Ritterbush, for example, forsook the Colorado rafting industry and moved his company, Whitewater Photography, to the New River Gorge in 1983. He still operates from Fayetteville today, selling photos of smiling, exhilarated raft customers at the campuses of all the major outfitters. If you've ever seen a picture of rafting on the New or Gauley Rivers before reading this book, the chances are decent that a Whitewater Photography employee took it.

He wasn't alone, however, in shooting visual images for long. In 1984, one of the most innovative companies on the water, Rivermen, pioneered the use of video for trip souvenirs. It was backbreaking work at the time to videotape a raft trip. There wasn't just a camera, which in and of itself was unwieldy. They also had to have a separate recording unit. Steve's brother, Brian, became one of the first whitewater videographers in the area and possibly anyplace.

When they first starting videoing, Brian and a friend began by running up the railroad tracks alongside the river to the Keeney's rapids, where they filmed the trip, and then ran back up to the tracks. They then ran to the next rapid and did it all again. "I remember passing the trip," said Brian. "We would get down there and have to do the white balance. We'd have sweat just pouring off. We'd get set up just in time to get the trip again, then pack it up, head up the trails and run down to pass them again before the next rapid!"

"That lasted a couple weeks," said Brian. "And then we got a trail bike." The trail bike worked well, but even it was not without snags. First of all, it was highly illegal to ride a motorbike up and down the CSX tracks, not to mention dangerous for both people and equipment. One cameraman left the bike parked on the tracks as he filmed, until he heard a train approaching. "He raced up the hill," said Brian, "and got there just in time, but he set the camera down in between the tracks. He got the bike off and then sat there and watched" as the train destroyed the camera.

At the end of their first videoed trip, the Campbells set up a television atop their van at the takeout and played the uncut footage for their guests. "And bam!" said Brian. "They just loved it."

In 1985, Steve decided that video would be best if done on the river rather than beside it. He became the first video boater—possibly in the world—when he began to shoot from a raft. "I got downstream at water level, and everything is coming at me," he said. "If one raft flips and those customers are in the water, the next raft is in the video and so is the next one. And there's the customer swimming toward you. Everything was in it." The approach was much more difficult than the way video boaters shoot today, from eddies or boulders alongside the water, but both Campbells agree the result was better.

Even early on in the industry's history, horseback riders, ATV riders, rock climbers and even pack mule outfitters worked with rafting companies at one point or another, evidencing a multi-activity trend that Rivers may have conceived but that likely would have started anyway. Indeed, though they weren't the first to contemplate a resort model, you won't find a person in the industry today that doesn't think ACE Adventure Resort implemented it the most successfully.

As early as the mid-1980s, ACE's Ernie Kincaid knew that aggressive growth would be one key to success, and indeed, ACE now owns licenses from several earlier companies. "We started ACE by meeting in a room at the old Chuckwagon Motel, which became the Whitewater Inn, which is now a senior citizens' home, I guess," said Kincaid. "Then Daryl Johnson, who owned WV Whitewater, let us meet at his place for a while."

Eventually, ACE bought a river camp in Thurmond, and its growth spurt, which appears to be never-ending, began. The company purchased property in the town of Glen Jean, which became its headquarters. During its time there, ACE also purchased three smaller companies: Hell and High Water, Whole Earth Ohio and Whole Earth WV.

When Imre Szilagyi and Appalachian Wildwaters expanded in 1985 and 1986 by purchasing companies in Tennessee, North Carolina and Texas, one of the owners he purchased from was Jerry Cook, who promptly took Szilagyi's money, bought a large share of ACE and began to compete with AW in West Virginia.

By then, ACE ran about eight thousand people per year down the two rivers, and its Glen Jean property was overflowing. "At the same time, we were merging with Whole Earth," said Kincaid, "and the primary owner there wanted us to buy the property we're on now. Everybody kind of liked the property, and to make the merger go, we went ahead and bought it—the central ninety-eight acres."

That property in Minden became the foundation upon which ACE would build the largest and most successful resort in the area. They sold their property at Glen Jean, which allowed them to build their first chalets. "The lodging is where the money is," said Kincaid. "The money's not in rafting. Just watch Adventures on the Gorge build as fast as they can. We told Dave Arnold years ago, 'Build chalets, Dave!'"

In more recent years, ACE purchased half of WV Whitewater at auction and a third of Drift-a-Bit and merged with both NARR and Jon Dragan's original company, Wildwater Unlimited.

But, said Kincaid, "the problem with the whitewater rafting industry is that people don't want to raft in the winter. I don't understand it," he chuckled, "but they just don't want to go. We're sitting there with fifty-one cabins, eleven bunkhouses, a lounge and dining rooms—and everything empty in the wintertime. So obviously, we've got to change that."

On the other side of the gorge, similar doings were afoot.

"It wasn't a secret to anybody at all in the industry that it was shrinking," said Paul Breuer of Mountain River Tours. Raft companies carry a huge amount of overhead, largely due to the fact that they cannot operate all year long in West Virginia, and over the course of years, Breuer and the boys from Class-VI had several informal discussions about joining forces. "We all recognized that if we merged and the numbers got up per outfit, then it was profitable again."

Discussions eventually became more serious. "Dave talked to me and said, 'Hey there's an opportunity here. What do you think?'" Breuer realized it was going to take a large amount of capital to put adventure vacations and West Virginia recreation back on the vacation map. "Singularly," he said, "the rafting wasn't *it* anymore. It was core, but not *it*. I recognized that the other people in this partnership were dedicated to the same things I was, and that's when I really felt that the opportunity was great."

As raft numbers continued to slide throughout the 1990s and into the new millennium, the industry shrunk in response, and not always painlessly. Overcapacity led to mass discounting and other practices to draw customers, but to little avail. Mostly, those outfitters only succeeded in making themselves less profitable. Some companies simply folded in response. Others sold their operations and permits to more growth-minded companies. Not everybody agrees that this change is for the best. Many look back fondly on simpler times, when there was the whitewater and nothing else really mattered. Ask a raft guide what he or she thinks is the most important key to a company's success and you'll likely hear: "The best raft trip."

Many of the owners and principals will disagree, though. "You can't be just a great outfitter anymore," said Dave Arnold emphatically. "You have to be a resort."

But even Arnold is not immune to the nostalgia of it all. He and pretty much every other raft company owner began their careers as guides,

A Wildwater raft emerges from the mist on Tumble Home, Gauley River, 1985. *Butch Christian Collection.*

and you just can't turn off that love of the river. "It was probably super healthy at the time for the industry to have, I think, thirty-seven permits at the height of it," he conceded.

"That was the generation that had this wanderlust that you don't see too much anymore," added Breuer.

ACE had been hard at work for years building an adventure resort, and leaping ahead of its competition, when Class-VI merged with Mountain River Tours and Rivermen. Paul Buechler led that merger and now serves as CEO of the conglomerate, Adventures on the Gorge. Buechler, himself a former raft guide, gave up his life as a successful financier to take an enormous pay cut and move to the gorge. That was not, however, his original intention. Buechler's first thought was to purchase Class-VI. But when he looked at the books, he immediately noticed that the profitability, especially into the future, seemed weak. He met with the owners and told them, "I can give you a number, but…if I told you what your business was worth, you'd probably say thanks for coming, but we're not interested." Instead, Buechler suggested a roll up—combining more than one company into a merger of two major players.

"It's like putting any family together," said Breuer. "There are always going to be bumps in the road and trials. But you learn, and hopefully you keep your core values in mind. That's got to be key to anything."

Today, there are still a few small outfitters around. Cantrell Ultimate Rafting seems to be experiencing a small amount of growth, while New and Gauley River Adventures still plies the river and quietly keeps to itself. North American River Runners sold to ACE after years of rumors, and Songer was alive and well until early 2011, when it finally agreed to sell its equipment and license to Adventures on the Gorge. Of course, Rivers, Extreme Expeditions and Appalachian Wildwaters are all part of River Extreme Adventure Resort now. West Virginia Adventures is still happily in operation, as is Alpine Ministries, an outfitter that caters to Christian families.

That's seven companies, from a heyday of thirty-seven, and life for small outfitters is unlikely to get easier. "If you don't have the capital to invest," said Buechler, "it's going to be harder to compete."

And yet, the outfitters' main competition continues to be, not one another or even other rafting destinations, but other types of vacations in general. West Virginia ski resorts in particular developed offerings that made them more like year-round outfitters than winter-only destinations. They added downhill mountain biking, for example, which continues to be a huge draw and allows them to rely less and less on ski revenue. "Our real competition is cruise ships, the beach and Disney," said Buechler. "This is the big enchilada because the market for seven-day vacations is huge. We don't need a very big piece of that market to be successful."

Will adventure tourism in and around the New River Gorge succeed long-term? There is some hope. Even as the industry as a whole continues to shrink, the resorts are growing thanks to increased lodging and activities other than rafting. Overall raft numbers were up in 2010 for the first time in many years, a sign that—just maybe—the long slide has leveled out.

The certain remaining obstacle appears to be that the industry as a whole has a public relations problem, namely that people don't know what an adventure resort is. "That's our challenge," pointed out Buechler, "to get people to realize what our value proposition is—what you get when you come to an adventure resort."

Epilogue

Sweet's Falls, Part II

Two years to the day after I sat atop Video Rock and watched the ultimate Sweet's Falls show unfold, I—a third-year raft guide—led my first professional trip down the Upper Gauley River.

I had a crew of large, strong men who were more than capable of pulling our fourteen-foot raft downstream and avoiding rocks along the way. It was my check-out run, which means I also had Tansy Ferguson, an experienced Gauley guide, aboard to judge my performance. My crew was on day two of a bachelor party weekend, and after a bouncy bus ride, a couple of them seemed pale around the gills. They swore they were raring to go, though. I certainly was.

By midday, we had successfully navigated almost all of the Upper Gauley's major rapids—running lines pioneered by the likes of the Rodmans and Paul Breuer. Only one big drop remained—Sweet's Falls. Looking back, the entire trip seems like a blur, except for Sweet's, most of which I remember as clearly as if I were running it right now.

We finished the rapid immediately upstream of Sweet's and drifted into a green pool under a huge cliff on the right bank. I took advantage of the lull to explain the rapid we were about to run. "This is Sweet's Falls," I said. "It's actually not so bad, if we're on our line. We're going to drift in along the right and take our time. I want this rapid to unfold slowly. If we get down there and we're not in the right place, I want as much time as possible to correct. When we go over the main drop, I'm going to yell 'Get down!' You know what to do then. Hit the floor. Hold onto your paddles."

"After the falls, don't pat yourself on the back. It won't quite be over," I continued. "We're going to move right around a big boulder called Postage Due. At that time, I'm going to angle the boat toward river left and call a few back strokes. That'll move us right." To a man, they nodded their understanding.

I further explained what to do if it all fell apart. "When I yell, 'Get down!' take a deep breath and hold it," I advised, "because if we miss to the right, it's going to be messy. If you swim, you might go deep, and you'll want that air. When you get up and get breathing again, I want you to swim to the right bank." I paused. "If we miss to the left, things may get, umm, *violent* for a moment, and we'll probably all be in the water. You won't have a lot of time, so when you get your bearings again, swim right *hard*. If you haven't already lost your paddle by then…what on earth were you thinking? Drop it and get moving." That got a nervous chuckle.

"This is the last of the big ones," I reminded them. "After this, we still have a ways to go, but all the really horrendous rapids will be behind us. We've had an amazing run so far, guys, and you've done a fantastic job moving the boat for me—in rapids far harder than this. Now, I need you one last time."

I was like a general rallying his troops for battle. My confidence was soaring, and I think, so was theirs.

"One last thing," I said. "This is the big stage." I thought of all those who guided Sweet's before me and, of course, of the carnage over the years. I wondered how many of its unfortunate victims had been in the same position I was in—on a check-out run with one big drop left to go. "As we move into this rapid," I continued, "you may notice that there are quite a lot of people lining the banks watching. They want us to screw up. They want us too far right or left. They want us in the water and terrified. I want you to ignore them. Pay them no attention. Focus on the task. Got it?"

"Got it," they replied. I risked a glance at Tansy, who studiously averted her gaze. I knew what she was thinking. *Don't F this up, Greenie. Don't put me in the water.* No pressure.

We drifted into the top ripples, and I could see the wave train that would carry us to the falls. I didn't want to be directly in the middle of those waves—that might put us too far right. We needed to get left a bit.

On either side of the river was land still owned by raft companies, and Sweet's Falls was a stadium packed with their customers, private boaters and hikers who had come solely to see the show. I looked right and saw people *everywhere*. They were even on the cliff above us wearing crazed, hungry grins. Never in my life did I feel so judged. I *couldn't* ignore them. They *demanded* my attention. There was no way to focus on anything but them.

I dragged myself kicking and screaming back into the moment. We were too far right, but it wasn't too late. I could adjust. I gave a little pry, pushing the back of the boat away from shore the tiniest amount. "One back!" I yelled over the growing roar of the river, and the crew dutifully back stroked once. The boat moved left just enough. I drew water toward me to straighten it. "One back!" I yelled again. They did so, and we slowed a bit. Slow was good.

I needed to see the spray bouncing off Dildo Rock to get a true bearing. *Where was it?* The current of my world ebbed to a trickle and the rapid slowed to a crawl. I could hear the roar of the river, and I could feel my heart pounding as the horizon loomed ever closer and Sweet's Falls opened up before and beneath us.

I'd love to go into detail about our how our run through Sweet's Falls ended, but oddly enough, it's about where the clarity of my memory blurs again. We made it through cleanly, but like much of history, the finest details are lost forever.

The history of rafting on the New and Gauley Rivers, though—what led us to now—is still there for us to see if we just turn around and look at it before we disappear around the next bend.

But then again, the now has a way of sneaking up on us, doesn't it, whether we pay mind to its course or not.

If you're fortunate enough to run these rivers, I hope you'll pay attention to the whole experience. There's a lot of history yet to be written, and sometimes, if we're lucky, we'll get to see a show.

BIBLIOGRAPHY

Bayes, Rick. *Whitewater Rafting Numbers 1994–2008*. Fayetteville, WV: Rick Bayes. 2008.

———. *Whitewater Rafting Numbers 2000–2010*. Fayetteville, WV: Rick Bayes. 2010.

Good, Gregory A., and Lynn Stasick. *New River Gorge National River Administrative History*. Washington, D.C.: U.S. National Park Service, 2008.

Lynn, Bob. "Wild Trip Down Wild River." *Enquirer*, May 3, 1970.

Marshall, John, et al. *River Commission Report*. Richmond, VA: Enquirer, February 1813.

Palmer, Tim. *Youghiogheny, Appalachian River*. Pittsburgh: University of Pittsburgh Press, 1984.

Rodman, Sayre. "The First Run." *Highlands Voice* 39, no. 12 (December 2006): 4–5.

Smith, Jean Edward. *John Marshall: Definer of a Nation*. New York: Henry Holt and Co., LLC, 1996.

Summersville TV and Eric Palfrey. *Paddles of the Past*. Video. Summersville, WV, 2008.

Taft, Susan L. *The River Chasers: A History of American Whitewater Paddling*. Mukilteo, WA: Flowing Waters Press and Alpen Books Press, 2001.

Trout, William E., III. *The New River Atlas: Rediscovering the History of the New and Greenbrier Rivers*. Lynchburg: Virginia Canals and Navigation Society, 2003.

Virgin, Bill. "Hydroelectricity Study by Corp Due This Month." *Charleston* [West Virginia] *Daily Mail*, October 15, 1981.

WV Wildwater Association. Letter to members entitled "Fellow Riverrunners." November 11, 1981.

Interviews

Arnold, Dave, Jeff Proctor and Bud Franz, December 9, 2010.

Breuer, Paul, January 6, 2011.

Buechler, Paul, March 11, 2011.

Casto, Kim, and Agnes Casto, March 13, 2011.

Ivey, Michael, January 19, 2011.

Neal, Michael, December 20, 2010.

Nibert, Larry, and Doug Ludwig, December 23, 2010.

Palfrey, Eric, January 12, 2011.

Proctor, Doug, November 3, 2010.

Proctor, Jeff, March 11, 2011.

Rahall, Nick, Congressman (D-WV, Third District), January 14, 2011.

Trout, William E., III, December 20, 2010.

Underwood, Bob, December 20, 2010.

Walbridge, Charlie, January 3, 2011.

Zoia, Jim, March 11, 2011.

ABOUT THE AUTHOR

Jay Young has lived in the New River Gorge area for five years and worked as a whitewater guide for three of them. When he's not running rivers or climbing rocks, he's a freelance writer in nearby Fayetteville and is closely connected to the local rafting community. He says, "My time on the back of a raft left me with a profound appreciation for the quirkiness of this sport, this industry and the people who ply it. (We're talking boatloads of quirk here.)"